SOUL

OF A

WOMAN

SOUL

—— OF A ——

WOMAN

HOW TO CULTIVATE BEAUTY, POWER AND PURPOSE
THROUGH UNDERSTANDING YOUR TRUE SOULFUL SELF

TINA MAJERLE

Star House
PUBLISHING

For any information regarding permission and bulk purchases contact:

www.starhousepublishing.com or email
info@starhousepublishing.com

ISBN PAPERBACK   978-1-989535-42-4
ISBN HARDCOVER   978-1-989535-43-1
ISBN E-BOOK   978-1-989535-44-8

Printed in the United States of America
First Edition, 2021.

Design by: Susanne Clark | Creative Blueprint Design
Edited by: Jackie Brown

To Madison, McKenzie, Mia, and Max:
my love for you is infinite.

CONTENTS

PART 3
MIND+BODY+SOUL=BEAUTIFUL

INTRODUCTION

*Authenticity is the daily practice of letting go of who
we think we're supposed to be and embracing who we are.*

—**Brené Brown**

Who am I and who do I want to be? Have you *ever* asked yourself
those questions?

As modern women, we are engaged in an epic internal war
fought on the battlefield of a fast-paced, hectic life. On one side,
we are compelled to balance stresses at work, raise ideal children,
be supportive of our significant others, and still somehow manage
to stay beautiful and sexy. On the other side of the battlefield, our

souls fight to protect us by trying to preserve autonomy and personal happiness.

Unfortunately, the outside world has a tendency to trample our souls' desires. Our war-torn, depleted souls raise white flags and shrink as we zealously strive to conform to what the world thinks is the best…the best mother, the best wife, the best employee…the best everything but our true selves. If we are lucky, we recognize the draining patterns. But far too often we find that contemplation of our own needs is nearly impossible as time and solitude are mere luxuries. We eventually become shells, caricatures, and shadows of our real selves. We then wonder, *who was I and who did I want to be?* We cannot even remember.

It is far too easy for women to be shackled to something or someone that holds us back from our true potential. It could be a difficult childhood, cold marriage, excess weight, or negative thinking. Whatever it is, lingering and sour energy spills over into every aspect of our lives. Toxicity manifests in ways diametrically opposed to our idea of being the best, and we end up with destructive romantic relationships, superficial friendships, weak connections to our kids, sick bodies, and defeated spirits.

Unless we truly know who we are inside and what we want out of life…unless we know our souls…we really cannot be the best anything. And not knowing our real selves will block us from achieving our full potential.

But hope is not lost. We can reclaim our souls and create lives that are healthier and more satisfying. All of us can become soulful women, and we can do this without shirking our jobs, kids, or spouses. This adjustment only means we will become genuine versions of ourselves.

So, how exactly will we transform into these miraculous people that are waiting inside of us? Just go back to the first two questions: *Who am I and who do I want to be?* The answers will guide you.

Chances are that we all want to be the type of woman who knows the healing power of forgiveness. We want the empowerment that comes from living a life filled with integrity and grace. We also want to be women who know that in order for relationships to flourish, we must first bring sensible intentions to them.

As we dig deep and transform, we strip away the sludge on the surface and get down to our true soulful selves. Also, we find answers to these questions:

- What do I value?
- What are my destructive patterns?
- How do I *really* see myself?
- Have I been living life with a graceful heart?
- What meaningful connections have I forged with others for a more productive life?

SOUL OF A WOMAN DEFINED

This is a woman who is mastering her intellectual, emotional, and physical natures while constantly striving to live her best life. A soulful woman is always in the process of mastering her existence. Life is not stagnant. Therefore, you will always have to gain more experience, grow, change, and evolve due to the constant ebb and flow of daily living. Moreover, a soul sister does not strive to attain anyone else's idea of a good life. She discovers and acts upon what is proper for her.

It was an event that happened early in my first marriage that shocked me and began my pursuit of knowledge into the importance of becoming a soulful woman. That event changed my whole perspective on how women betray themselves and end up damaging their souls, that eternal essence that connects them to the Higher Power. While they self-sabotage, it is not surprising they are ignorant to the reverberating impacts on other women, their soul sisters, and the children of those sisters.

A man I knew well walked into a social gathering with a beautiful young woman on his arm. She was not his wife and their relationship to each other was obvious. As a fellow woman, I was puzzled by her obvious pride. I could see that a woman who was proud to be on the arm of a married man is lost and chasing a type of joy that is not eternal, and is, in so many ways, karmically damaging. Right there in that restaurant I vowed to write a book and that it would be for women, for our souls, and our sisterhood.

Admittedly, I was guilty of not being a master of my own life by letting my past and others define what was right for me. I had gone through a rough time that left me feeling insecure and helpless. In order to avoid pain, I learned how to survive in that world by becoming what others wanted me to be. But these efforts to ignore the cries of my aching soul came out in troubling anxiety attacks and poor self-esteem.

Fortunately, two things pulled me through one of the most gut-wrenching times of my life. First, my treasured friends came to my rescue and became my rock. And second, a Bible study group restored my faith in God. If it were not for my "girls" embracing me and showing me how to find faith in myself and the unfailing grace of God, I do not know if I would be strong enough to write these words now. In the end, I became a soul sister and found the resolve to become a more competent and confident mother. I worked on healing myself and gaining more peace of mind.

At the time, my priority was my own marriage and raising my kids, but as my kids grew more independent, I turned to the work that would lead to writing this book. I started reading the Bible in a more intellectual way and even read the key books of other religions. I spent a lot of time reading important texts on Buddhism. I studied positive psychology and I took private writing courses. With all this investment in learning and growth, I became proficient at understanding my thoughts, understanding the mind and human behavior, and at getting my processed thoughts on paper.

One of my key revelations was that women need to find a purpose and follow their intrinsic value in order to find a lasting and eternal joy. When you are looking for purpose and happiness and believe that you will do anything to get it—are willing to sell your soul and break someone else's—there is something rotten in that mental and spiritual transaction. What you will get is not eternal joy. The woman who sparked something within me to examine soulful women, despite her appearance of joy, was not seeing the full effects of what she was doing. She was happy to be on the arm of someone at that moment, at the cost of her connection to her soul. And that is a great part of what I seek to rebalance in women through my work and through this book.

Thus, the reasons I have written this book are three-fold:

1. It is an open thank you to my soul sisters, who while we may unintentionally hurt each other as we learn and grow, we have never let each other down.

2. I want to let other women who find themselves in a crisis know they are not alone as they try to figure out who they are and who they want to be.

3. I want this book to be a guide to help women understand what the soul is and its importance in their connection to the Higher Power, whether they call that power God, or by another name. The soul is our eternal essence. It is what plugs us into God. It is pure and always remains untouched by the rigors of this world.

This book is a comprehensive plan that focuses on three areas that by choice and circumstance forced me to grow into a more accomplished person. I want this for you. The three areas are:

- The Self
- Relationships
- Mind + Body + Soul = Beautiful

By embracing and working on these areas, we will steadily make our way toward the peace and harmony we desire and deserve. We will no longer be defined by the fickleness of life circumstances but instead will redefine them from within. This positive inner change will eventually manifest an outward form we can be proud of. After all, we have the power to choose our highest good.

The journey toward becoming our most stellar selves starts only in one place—with us. However, we should not take this trip lightly. As we set off, the road will be filled with hills that we have to climb, abysmal potholes, and constant roadblocks in the form of negative thoughts that are detrimental to our well-being. It will be filled with self-doubt, not to mention the many unforeseen obstacles that will hound us. The passage will not be quick and definitely not easy. But I have faith that we will trudge on and reach a point where the road is smooth and flat, striding confidently towards our final destination.

PART
—1—

THE SELF

CHAPTER 1

SOUL CHILD

Turn your wounds into wisdom.

—Oprah Winfrey

The concept of God is wholly personal. You can choose to experience God as the ultimate creator, a rarefied spiritual energy, the higher self, the universe, or an excellent state of mind. But no matter how you perceive God, we will define the soul as the creative truth which seeks to bring forth only the perfection of God in human beings.

Our souls are perfectly made, possessing all the goodness of the heavenly kingdom they descended from. Souls are pieces of God's spirit that guide us and act as reminders of His love. Practically speaking, souls are what help us put into practice the God-given wisdom we've been innately gifted with.

Since humans possess souls, we are created flawless. However, from the moment of birth, we can be conditioned to act in ways diametrically opposed to our own good. Programmers can include our parents, immediate environment, culture, and other stimuli. Though their negative programming is often unintentional, it can still have unfortunate effects.

For instance, like most people, my father was one of my programmers. Many people thought he was quite funny, but when he was younger, his manner was similar to a Mafia-embroiled gangster on the television show *The Sopranos*. I saw him as tough and aggressive. Rough around the edges. This affected how I viewed myself as I was of his blood. Thus, I did not feel flawless. I felt others would judge me based on the stereotypes of Italians I saw portrayed in the media and which seemed reinforced by my own father's behavior. I fought against any association with my Italian heritage. However, my family wanted me to be proud of being Italian, but with my warped view that was not possible.

As we mold ourselves into what is expected of us by our programmers, our souls call out to try to guide us back home. But our acquired programming prevents us from hearing them. We end up in conflict with others, who are also not following the guidance of their own souls. It took a visit to Italy to change my opinion and heal this aspect of my soul. Away from the American context, I saw my fellow Italians as gracious, peaceful, and loving; I wept as I accepted a new version of the Italian in me and forgave myself for all the judgments I had carried. I later took my children to Italy to ensure they would gain a better perspective of our heritage so that they would not grow up with the any harmful misconceptions.

Challenging situations like internal judgment destroy the commonality and harmony we'd have without the mixed messages from our programmers. This is why forgiveness is so important. It is a way for the soul to manifest in reality by outwardly spreading inner peace. *Forgiveness also allows us to have the understanding that we all have the capability to hurt one another or fall from grace.* This point will be brought up again; so, do remember it.

But forgiveness isn't easy. It takes maturity, depth of character, and an understanding of the miracle that we are all truly united by the spirit. That is why learning to forgive takes time and many lessons. Our souls are our teachers and present themselves in the form of our individual soul child, which we'll now explore.

FOREVER YOUNG

"Why don't you just grow up" is a criticism given to certain adults who refuse to comply with the expectations and responsibilities of adulthood. And why would they? It's so much more fun to live a Peter Pan-type life. Being mature requires us to adopt selfless, productive, and intelligent behaviors. However, those who refuse to grow up tend to be menaces to society with their insolent moods and parasitic personalities. No one would ever advocate becoming one of them.

But what if there is a part of us that should never grow up? There is, you know. It's the part of the soul that keeps reminding us of our purity and innocence—the soul child. The soul child is a conglomeration of all the spiritual goodness we're born with. We all start our incarnations in that beautiful and wonderfully made state.

The soul child is malleable, having the ability to constantly grow and become wiser, and yet it remains pure. Also, the soul child always maintains its connection to our Divine Creator, and this spiritual link is a key component to living life to the fullest.

The soul child's innocence and purity can save us from being weighed down by present-day fears or past burdens, if we remember and let it. Innocence and purity allow us to see every situation with fresh eyes and inspire us to gravitate toward all things excellent. Put another way, you can think of innocence and purity like two smiley faces on the soul.

Remaining conscious of the soul child can be difficult at times, though. Some of us have been battered by so many harsh blows in life that we have lost touch with it all together. As time passes, the memory of what it was like to be whole seems like a dream. Some way, somehow, we have to get back to where we were before.

Though accumulated experiences and choices seem to taint our perfection, the soul child can be reclaimed. This means we will have to perform a balancing act. We'll have to allow ourselves to exist as "imperfect" humans and still somehow get back to the soul child within.

We do this by having a clear view of what reality is. Reality is truth. Though we have different perceptions of facts that we mislabel as truth, genuine truth stands on its own and does not change due to circumstances. We can argue and defend facts, but the truth has no counterpoint.

The truth is that creation had a starting point. Throughout existence all things came from that starting point called God; hence, we're part of Him. Identifying with this aspect of our being will grant us peace. However, while we're in bodies, we often forget who we really are and don't accept our goodness because life in this realm is often not conducive to re-affirming our inborn inheritance—the spirit of God.

When our forgetfulness is combined with material phenomenon, we may find it difficult to let go of our human definitions of what life is all about, especially when we've done everything right on a human level and things still seem to fall apart. These difficult times are the very events that will tempt us to disown our soul child.

But what if those very events and choices lead us to our ultimate good? Going through emotional or toxic avenues may be just the stimuli to reconnect us to our soul child. Difficult circumstances can make us determined to protect that pure innocence.

Instead of letting the innocence fade away, let's start approaching harsh situations with a different mindset. The improved mindset understands that what "happens" is not nearly as important as the response. If you choose to hold on to the worn-out and sad parts of your life, your soul child will transform from a youth to a crone. However, if you decide to focus on positive outcomes, your soul child will sparkle.

No matter your choice, you can take comfort knowing that your soul child never judges your flawed humanity and is ever ready to assist you when you need it the most. Don't hesitate to let it guide you through the awesomely transformative process of becoming a better human than you were yesterday.

ÉLAN VITAL

Élan vital is an energy within you that is responsible for your transformation.

The soul child is resistant to the taint of the outside world, preferring the lofty nature of existence. It possesses spiritual intelligence and has all the answers to our most profound questions. Therefore, the soul child is always ready to see, accept, and give Godly love. However, subtleness makes it sometimes *appear* to be more of an observer than an active participant in our lives.

But the soul child is not alone. It shares the body with another internal force called the inner child. Even though it's not the spirit, the inner child is an animating principle that is concerned with the intellectual and emotional aspects of a human being—basically consciousness. Without it, the body would be alive, but it would be an empty shell. It is also charged with day-to-day tasks and interactions with other people.

Unlike the soul child, the inner child is more about brain input rather than spiritual. Sometimes it's logical but can be terribly instinctive, especially when it feels like it's in any sort of danger. Though the inner child has moments of lucidity, with the reliance on instincts, it can be morose and reactive, even when no real danger is present. This is due to the influence of the ego and its desire for self-preservation at any cost.

But we shouldn't seek to destroy the inner child because it is needed to function in the material world. Instead, we must recognize that the inner child is immature when it's listening to the ego instead of the soul child. My interpretation of élan vital is that it is our responsibility to guide and heal the inner child with knowledge from the soul child. As the soul child is called forth and utilized, it releases the inner child from the grips of the ego and the poor conditioning and sense of shame that tags along with it. In time, the inner child will be transformed into a positive force that helps obtain happiness.

THE HURT INNER CHILD

The inner child is delicate and its state of being is dependent on the choices you make. The choices are the result of the opinions you have about yourself and the outside world.

Unlike the soul child, the inner child is easily affected by the whims and follies of outside forces. The inner child is always scanning the environment and listening to a voice telling it what is going on. That voice will either be that of the soul child or the ego. When overwhelmed by external circumstances, the inner child usually switches its attention from the quiet wisdom of the soul child to the loud and incomplete knowledge of the ego.

As I mentioned before, my ego sought to put a distance between my behavior and the media stereotypes of Italians. Thus, my inner child was confused by my opinions about Italians and the knowledge that I was one.

Under stress, the inner child tends to believe that the false self (the ego) is more reliable than the soul child. The inner child believes its current circumstances will be a permanent reality of duress as opposed to a temporary situation that can be changed with the assistance of the soul child. This information isn't meant to encourage anyone to live in a fantasy, pretending that circumstances aren't happening. What it does mean is that the essence of the circumstance may not be easy to comprehend and may actually have a useful purpose. Even though some stressful circumstances may be caused by the ego, others may be prompted by the soul as it processes information it needs in order to encourage change.

Making efforts to deal with emotions, positive thinking and mantras can offer real benefits. Here are some examples:

I am safe.
I am loved.
I am worthy.

Fear is a way the ego influences the inner child. Fear, like depression, is an internal state based on faulty perception. It places us in a non-existent future that's filled with despair and punishment. Moreover, these fears are based on the conditioning and trauma of past experiences that have not been released from the mind. Fear causes us to focus more on what has gone wrong rather than what has gone right, and we make predictions based on that.

The inner child tries its best to maintain balance, but it winds up fulfilling the ego's agenda by living a life dedicated to anxiety and prevention of future tragedy. But the phantom of fear cannot be outrun. Escape mechanisms like addictions to food or other destructive coping methods to suppress fear can offer fleeting relief. But these are tools of the ego. The ego is bent on using distractions in an effort to ensure its own survival. The last thing the ego wants is for us to go to our soul child because that would be the ego's death.

Now, in this world the inner child is going to be tested. This is how you grow stronger spiritually. But the outcomes of those tests are based on choice, and even though the full power of the soul child is activated by us choosing it, the soul child still seeks to help us, even when we ignore it. The soul child comes in the form of intuition and through the conscience. In times of challenge and frustration, it's the little voice that tells us to what to do. Its suggestions are usually opposite of what the ego is telling us to do at that very moment.

The ego's solutions require minimum effort. They usually make us feel better for a short time or give us the ability to be victorious at the expense of someone else. In other words, the ego's way consumes us with pride and gives an easy way out. For instance, in order to feel good about myself, it was easiest to shun everything that was Italian. I was not acknowledging who I was, as due to my ego, I was ashamed of being Italian. However, the soul child is humble, and the actions it recommends will require the mind to develop strength of character and submission to higher ideals. Siding with the soul child who is flawless and reminds us that we are made in God's image is the more difficult choice and requires commitment as it is a lifelong process. When you are living with the ego running things, you are living in a kind of hell.

But the soul child's heaven is so much better than the ego's hell. It's the place where the enemy cannot invade, and you can feel safe like a child in its mother's womb. The soul child gives us spiritual nourishment through the umbilical cord linked to God. You are fed a new perspective and strength to handle life's challenges by being responsive instead of reactive. Moreover, the soul child always makes us feel more optimistic and brings a sense of relief despite what is happening outside of us. It makes you remember that you are good enough and worthy of your connection to God. When this miracle happens, you fully trust God and are able to find the happiness that had been eluding you—happiness not based on externals but the truth.

Though the soul child does not guarantee a pain-free life, it does give the inner child access to the truth which is made of peace and joy. That truth allows us to express the wonderment of the soul and stop focusing on the circumstances brought about by life and the ego. We can see past the muck to an existence that reflects the glory of the God as He works through the soul child. This purity flows down to the inner child and allows it to deal with our earthly needs and obligations in the most proficient way possible.

THE "F" WORD

One of the soul child's greatest gifts is also one of its biggest challenges.

Unforgiveness is by far one of the fiercest tools the ego uses to keep us shackled in a solitary prison. True, the chains are not made of iron or steel, and we aren't looking through a depressing span of black bars. The demanding guards at this prison of our own making force us to constantly look over our shoulders for ghosts of past transgressions—ones either we committed or were visited upon us.

The key ring to the prison cell is within our reach. And there is one key on that ring. It's called forgiveness. Forgiveness is the gift that liberates us from the past. It keeps us forward focused with lightened hearts rather than being tethered to depression, angst, and vengeful plots.

So, attention! Your life—right here, right now—isn't a practice drill. You can never request a do-over and get one. This is it. One life. Some days that life may seem pretty long and to be moving at a snail's pace. But if you talk to someone on their deathbed, they'll confess how life ran past them faster than a blink.

Do you want to waste time clinging to negative events that no longer exist? What good has holding on to a sorrowful past brought you? Does that uplift you or cause you pain? You already know the answer.

We all have a choice. We can choose forgiveness or let the past turn us into tart, contemptible women. Our souls will compel us to choose the former. Souls know that life just happens, good and bad, and that it's all because of a bigger plan.

C.S. Lewis said it best: *Everyone thinks forgiveness is a lovely idea, until they have something to forgive.* One of the biggest tests we all go through is how to forgive terrible, even heinous, things that happened to us. But sometimes we use events or perpetrators as easy scapegoats for our failings. We blame them quietly in our heads as we brood over their sins or become aggressively vocal against them if we are particularly bold. But no matter how much we hurl guilt, the past still remains the same.

The soul child knows that pain doesn't have to last forever or bind us to the improper conditioning of the ego. It also knows that forgiveness is needed to lighten the heart. But we have to make the choice to dissolve the ego's influence and transform into the confident, well-rounded adults we want to be. After we choose forgiveness, the soul child steps in and will guide us down the path of letting go.

Forgiveness is not impossible; it's done every day. Take comfort in knowing that this world is filled with happy, successful, and well-adjusted people who had difficult pasts. We can all become one of them if only we choose to stop giving our power away to things we cannot change. We have to divest and stop holding on to what we don't need. Imagine the relief we'll feel when we stop carrying pain and let the heavy weight of it lift off our hearts.

Stop clanging cups against the bars of prison cells. It's time for a reprieve.

WHAT IS FORGIVENESS?

The ego's two minions, depression and fear, have an undercurrent of unforgiveness—a profound desire for the past to be different than what it was and the helplessness to change it. That is why the soul child uses forgiveness as a way to help us cross the abyss from impossibility to sanity, and of course, that's a lovely thought. But here's the deal with forgiveness: most of the time, we really just don't want to do it.

The inner child that is under the dictates of the ego would rather hold a grudge and wants some good, old-fashion revenge. The more terrible the offense, the more the ego tells the inner child that its seething, fiery rage is justified. The ego says that it is wrong to forgive, to release ourselves from the pain.

"Look at what they did to you…something must be done!" the ego screams. What the ego is saying *feels* right and vengeance seems like a powerful action to take. After all, someone did hurt us or someone we care about, sometimes in the worst of ways. So great was the pain they caused, we think it might be easier to die than endure it. Why should we forgive something like that?

But the thing is that we have to forgive because it frees us from bondage. Though it may seem like our unforgiving attitudes are somehow punishing the other person, we really put ourselves in a dark box where we can feel separated from our souls. Trapped, we're blocked from experiencing the delight we would've had if we had not embraced a calloused heart or given energy to pain. However, it's so hard to break out of the box based upon the common misperceptions about what forgiveness is.

Forgiveness is not:
- Something we do for someone else
- A process that always feels good
- Gives absolution to the offender
- Something that needs to happen one time

- Makes us forget what happened
- Creates a bond between us and the offender
- Done only if the offender is contrite
- Given only if the offense was not severe

Forgiveness really is:
- Not based on the severity of the offense
- At times, a herculean task
- Something we may have to do multiple times for a one-time offense
- Given whether the offender takes responsibility for their actions or not
- An understanding that the offender is still culpable for their actions, and if warranted, they should be held accountable for what they did (the criminal court system or divorce are examples)
- Not a guarantee of permanency for the relationship
- A decision that forgiveness saves our souls

The soul child is always ready to assist us when we seek to move on from the past. It knows how the offense robbed us of peace and sanity. But we're not forgiving a perpetrator; we're forgiving a child of God. And like us, those offenders have their own soul child. Therefore, on some level, we're one in the same. Forgiving them is forgiving an aspect of us. We can then see and understand their weaknesses. As terrible as the grievance was, they were only doing the best they could with the understanding that they had at that time. That's why forgiveness is really not about benefiting the offender, but it's about benefiting us.

Of course, evil must be dealt with. But pure evil is rare. Most of us will never have to confront and forgive pure evil. Most of our forgiveness tests come from our loved ones or other people we have frequent contact with. Their offenses usually revolve around disrespect, some form of abuse, or dishonesty. In those cases, there are steps we can take regarding forgiveness.

Let's start with prayer. When it's hard to forgive someone, sometimes the only thing to do is pray for them. To be clear, prayer cannot be thought of as some magic wand that will allow us to bewitch someone else's behavior or an outer event. In fact, when prayer is used for forgiveness, the other person or situation may not change at all. This is because we may be the one in need of change, and a forgiveness prayer always causes change at some level. Usually, it will soften us so that we release anger and resentment while helping us yield enough to allow growth to occur.

However, the softening and release of anger do not forbid confrontation. Sometimes we may have to confront someone about their behavior toward us; this serves to rattle existing conditions. The ego can discourage this, especially if the person is someone we care about. This is because there is a built-in risk that we will be rejected. No one wants to be abandoned by someone they care about simply for speaking up and establishing boundaries. The prospect of alienation can be terrifying, and the ego knows this. The ego uses avoidance as a way to keep the inner child dependent on it.

We also can distance ourselves from someone, or we remove them from our lives all together if they choose to continue their disruptive or harmful ways. However, ultimately, there is a choice that has to be made; it is not their choice but ours. We shouldn't be expected to subvert our own goodness in favor of their negative behavior; we must choose to honor and protect our souls.

While separating, if tempted to go back to dysfunction, we must remember that people will ultimately only treat us the way the ego has conditioned us to let them. That's why the power of exercising choice is so important. The soul child will never suggest that we abdicate our right to set clear boundaries regarding how we want and deserve to be treated. If anyone treads on those boundaries, we don't have to be a victim and can leave them behind. But no matter how we choose to deal with the situation, we still have to forgive. As a result, we'll not suppress or repress any harmful emotions. Also, our positive energy can go out into the world before us and reflect back our good decision when we meet it again through another person.

Shifting perspectives is rarely easy. Habits and conditioning have a way of keeping the inner child stuck on a seesaw of inertia and ineffective action. Sometimes it is more comfortable to maintain the destructive pattern of unforgiveness. Choosing to walk another path by forgiving someone nearly always produces discomfort as we believe that unforgiveness is gifting us with *something.* That *something* can be anything such as righteous indignation, the ability to justify our need for vengeance, or to have an excuse to fall back on when we fail in our own endeavors. But negative emotions and actions never bring us happiness. The only satisfaction resentment gives us is the delusion that the offender is the only one who is destroyed by it. But resentment kills its owner's mind, body, and soul as it blocks the flow of God's grace. Forgiveness, however, gives life. It is the healing power that mends the angry mind, broken soul, and aching heart.

Forgiveness is a conscious choice that can only be utilized when put into action. Mental (and sometimes physical) effort must be used in this process of transformation. That means ignoring impulses that would have us act opposite of what a loving God would have us do.

While practicing forgiveness, the lower nature will speak loudly and convincingly, encouraging you to follow through on ill-advised thoughts and activities. It will tell you that forgiveness is useless, that it is better to be a bitter victim. The tempting whisperings will tell you that feeling bad actually feels good and to maintain a sour view of the past. However, if you want an enhanced existence, you must make every effort to ignore those harmful thoughts.

Positive and mindful choices generated by the soul child are always superior to negative and reactive choices. This is because good choices put us in a prime position to actively affect outcomes as opposed to letting bad choices bring us so-called destined events. Redirecting bad choices based on the past only takes a change in perspective. And that change in perspective is usually a result of forgiveness.

Hope for a future with a positive purpose and creative mindfulness are products of forgiveness. These encourage a more meaningful life that is worth living through joyful times as well as struggles. Unfortunate circumstances then become life-enhancing learning events that encourage us to make better choices in the future. Moreover, positive solutions to today's current problems will be easier to make because you refuse to be stuck in the sadness of the past.

KINDS OF FORGIVENESS

There are two types of forgiveness—external and internal. External forgiveness is given to persons and situations outside of oneself, and internal forgiveness is forgiving yourself.

31

EXTERNAL FORGIVENESS

When someone hurts us, sometimes our immediate reaction is to hurt them back. We may believe their guilt relieves us of any responsibility we may have in the situation, squarely placing all blame on them. This can actually make us feel vindicated and superior, and the rush of adrenaline is real. However, a cocoon of hubris offers false comfort.

While resentment may have a legitimate cause, we are concerned with how unforgiveness and the worship of condemnation affect the soul. Buddha said, *Holding on to anger is like grasping a hot coal with the intent of throwing it at someone else; you are the one who gets burned.*

Think about it. How has being bitter made life any better? Physically, holding on to bitterness raises stress hormones and damages the body. Bitterness also ages the body and makes it send out signals that put others off. On the mental level, it causes corrosion of personal happiness and an unpleasant attitude.

The inverse of outward blame is feeling shame or fear for having unforgiving thoughts in the first place. So instead of pointing the finger, we act like we aren't bothered, internalize, and become depressed. Or we try to maintain the status quo because we receive some benefit, and we fear losing it. Then again, if the memory of the event is too painful to deal with, we actively try to forget…which never works… and some form of post-traumatic stress syndrome develops. There is no way we can be unforgiving and have a truly joyful existence at the same time.

It's time to make a new start by getting rid of the notion that forgiveness is about saying it was okay for someone else to hurt us. At the same time, if the offender is willing, let him make amends for his wrongdoing. This type of justice is reparative as opposed to being vindictive. However, after the offender has made amends, it is appropriate to restore him by giving him the chance to do better. This second chance is to be given without hatred or feelings of moral superiority. That is called mercy—mercy for them, but it is also mercy for us.

Forgiving others is not about saving someone else's soul; it is about saving our own. The trick is to eliminate the idea that we should not *have* to experience pain, that somehow, we should be exempt. Once we get that out of the way, then forgiveness can be used as a tool to help us as we learn to work through all of life's distressing circumstances and become empathetic toward our Judases. After all, most of us don't reject the idea of forgiveness. It's only when we try to put it into action that we encounter mental blocks. To help with that, here are some practical ways we can move toward forgiveness:

Be "okay" with how we feel: It's absolutely normal to feel hurt or agony by what someone did to us, and if we aren't ready to change that just yet, we don't have to. However, if our negative feelings affect our lives in destructive ways, we're going to have to forgive at some point. Forgiveness is not pretending the offense didn't happen. Forgiveness is making the decision that the event will not ravage us from the inside out.

Journal through it: We can write down all the hurts, disappointments, and pain we think someone else gave us. This will be easy, especially if we are in blame mode. But we should try to go past emotionalism and stay as centered as possible. After that's done, we look at our particular gripe list. It will probably be quite long. Next, we *really* look at it and then proceed to remove all the trivial slights and leave only the things that cut the core.

Process how those events and people made us feel: Is there hate in our hearts for our parents or some other relative who did us wrong? Is there some affront being chewed over that happened years, maybe decades ago? Once we get past the anger, state the real feelings. Do not be surprised if "disappointed" and "helpless to do anything" are at the top of the list.

Turn the pain around and write a blessing received from it: The blessing could be just recognizing the situation and releasing it at that moment. Maybe events that caused heartache were part of an evolutionary process that gave specific life lessons or the gift of wisdom that could be passed on to others. Blessings are not always easy to see. It's our job to seek them out and unearth the peace, joy, and knowledge that the past had in it. Miracles are delivered during times of discomfort, to give us the opportunity to find the grace within ourselves and others through the power of forgiveness. It's only then, do we find true happiness.

Whenever the memory of a past event and unforgiveness crop up, ask: Is the event still happening? If not, stop nursing the pain and move on.

Remember we've all caused someone sorrow, be it a small infraction or grievous error: Somewhere in our lifetimes, we've done or said something that generated suffering for another, possibly resulting in a negative chain-reaction we aren't even aware of. Therefore, we need forgiveness, too. Calling to mind our own desire for forgiveness can create a genuine sense of empathy toward the "offender" and help us move from anger to peace.

Enjoy all the wonderful things in our lives right now: At this very moment, we're surrounded by so many gifts; so, we shouldn't get stuck in the past. We can now be thankful for good things like our homes, careers, the ability to be of service to others, and that God allowed us to even have bodies to experience life in, the good and the bad.

INTERNAL FORGIVENESS

Though both forms of forgiveness take some effort, internal forgiveness is often the more difficult of the two. This stems from our own need for vengeance against others. When someone else performs an infraction, our first thought is that they need punishment, and if that punishment is not delivered, we feel as though justice has not been served. Sadly, often it is only when retribution is delivered, or we have given out false forgiveness, that we think balance has been restored.

But what happens if we are at fault and we have to forgive ourselves? It seems disingenuous. After all, who can absolve themselves, especially if they worship revenge and punishment? Those who don't believe in absolution can go on to perform nefarious self-harming activities, consciously or unconsciously. The self-flogging is real but never erases the deed or brings a sense of forgiveness. In fact, self-harm creates more situations that we'll have to forgive ourselves for. Since escape can't be found in guilt, we have to find ways to move on. We can:

Stop obsessing over the past: Since we're our own worst critics, we ruminate over what we should have done or said. We want to go back to the past and change it because we feel like our goodness was swallowed up by our mistakes. But the realization sets in that we can't go back, and the only way to cope is to suppress the guilt. This guilt makes us prone to physical breakdowns and mental health issues like obsessive compulsive disorder, anxiety, panic attacks, and other forms of self-abuse. That's why even when someone else gives us their forgiveness, it still doesn't matter. We still grieve over failing ourselves. Instead, we should redirect our thoughts to the present moment and make every effort to do better.

Ignore the ego: While the guilty ego argues against it, forgiveness of self is a must. We cannot be of service to anyone else if we are riddled with self-condemnation. We must re-conceptualize our past mistakes. Even though there were other choices, we only did what we could do with the understanding, bravery, and maturity we had at the time.

Use a different vision: We now have hindsight, and that gives us power. However, this newfound power can only be accessed with a clear conscience, free from self-attack. We can start by uncovering and working through our biggest regrets.

Regret only for a short time: Temporary regret is not a bad thing. It actually validates that we are good people because we have the ability to feel remorse. Temporary regret makes us do better and reminds us of our values. But our biggest regrets are the ones that make self-forgiveness extremely difficult. We may have tried to distance ourselves from the mistakes, and it feels terrible to call them to mind. However, we must move past regret, or it will become pathological.

Be responsible: We go on to being responsible for the consequences. Those consequences can make it hard to self-forgive because they may have resulted in harsh or even devastating circumstances. We cannot go back in time, so we must accept responsibility for what happened. Acceptance may never feel good, but that's not its purpose. Acceptance is there to simply help us move along.

Know that it's okay to make mistakes: We just have to learn and grow from them. And through learning, we are not the same people we were before. We have changed for the better. New positive behavior patterns make us greater.

Keep faith in ourselves: When it comes to making mistakes, try to remember that we're in good company. Everyone has done something they wish they could take back. These people are our parents, children, friends, clergy…the list goes on. If these people can make mistakes and we haven't turned our backs on them, there is no need to turn against ourselves.

BUT WHAT IF I REALLY CAN'T FORGIVE?

Even with the sincerest desire to forgive, it can be all but impossible to accomplish for some. The ego is particularly strong in those cases. Is there a stopgap measure to utilize when your ability to forgive is practically nonexistent? Well, try this exercise:

Visualize yourself writing down all the painful details of an unforgivable event. When finished, imagine walking over to a gigantic, hungry paper shredder. Say, "I am choosing to let you go now. I have no need to keep you in my heart. I choose to forgive (name the person or event) and say goodbye to the past." Then feed the paper with past woes into the shredder. See the pieces ripped apart until they reach atomic size and disappear. Keep performing this visualization until a more substantial forgiveness state occurs.

HOW WILL I KNOW I HAVE FORGIVEN?

If you've truly forgiven, you'll not even have to ask that question. However, for information's sake, you'll know that you've forgiven when you remember the event or are confronted with the person that you had a grievance against and no longer have any venom in your heart. You basically feel neutral.

RECONNECTING TO THE SOUL CHILD

Now that we know how to overcome the obstacle of unforgiveness, we can work on our connection to the soul child. Since the soul child resides within, it is mostly going to interact with us from that place. However, sometimes the soul child will try to connect to you by using some external source.

The soul child will often use synchronicities to communicate with you; so be aware of these Godwinks. Synchronicities are coincidences that seem to come when you need an answer to a question. They can also be highly symbolic signs directing you to take some action. Sometimes they are just random occurrences that the soul uses to let you know it's there.

Dreams are another way the soul child talks to you. Sometimes in dreams the soul child gives some much-needed information or some comfort regarding events going on at that moment. Like synchronicities, dreams are often symbolic, so they must be interpreted based on your personal ideas.

The soul child meets you at your current level of understanding and only gives information that you are ready to receive and use at the time. The more the soul child's advice is followed, the more it gives. Eventually, the soul child will merge with the inner child. When that happens, multiple benefits are received.

First, there's healing. This includes emotional, physical, and psychological healings. The soul child only knows how to make a person strong in every way. It wants us to be emotionally stable, healthy, and able to use our intellects to make progress through life. The soul child, when given permission, will mend the parts of our lives that are suffering. Then, rather than feeling like victims, we are able to work with what has happened and use it to our benefit.

Second, abundance shows up. Do not get caught up with the idea of material possessions or money. Remember, the soul child is not a deliverer of excess and does not support greed. But it does want us to have an abundance of all the good that God has to offer. The soul child knows exactly what is needed to be happy. Therefore, we must not base our joy on desires created by our egos. After all, abundance comes in many forms like love, peace, and sometimes material goods. But even when material or financial windfalls occur, the soul child may have made it available to be shared with others.

Fulfillment is the third benefit. When the soul child and inner child work together, they help us stop grasping for external things to satisfy us. At the same time, we'll not be resigned to living an unwanted life because the soul child directs us to what's best for us. Those blessings will always be pleasing if only we recognize them as being gifts. We'll have contentedness and can relax in the peaceful existence we've been longing for.

The fourth benefit is equanimity. Troubling situations will no longer rev us up. We are able to deal with difficult circumstances with composure and grace. We become the calm center when others are afraid. Our mental balance will provide much needed assurance for them. This will also enable us to be effective leaders by allowing us to make clear and thoughtful decisions based on logic rather than fear or other negative emotion.

And finally, there's the benefit of greater creative intelligence. Creative intelligence is not the same as pure intellect. Pure intellect can be manipulated by the ego. Pure intellect is based on left-brain thinking and is concerned with facts, science, math, or other concrete thought processes. A person with pure intellect often can spout off stats or recall a great deal of trivial information. Moreover, though pure intellect gets things done, it is often concerned with personal gain. However, creative intelligence uplifts not only our thinking but everyone else's as well. It has the ability to create beauty which is a display of love. Ideally, the soul child seeks to incorporate both intelligences inside of us.

Regardless of our past decisions, today we have the choice to be exactly who we want to be. It is a victim's way out to blame current failures on anything that happened yesteryear or to rely on a damaged ego. The only value the ego has is to teach us where we don't want to go. Falling is inevitable. However, we'll all have another chance to get back up because the future is constantly creating itself.

SOUL AFFIRMATION

Forgiveness is not about forgetting or giving absolution to the unredeemable. Forgiveness is simply my willingness to face the pain. It does not matter if I received the pain or gave it. I choose to let the pain go and put hopefulness and cheer in its place. Shame and guilt no longer lead me.

CHAPTER 2

SOUL PURPOSE

A woman should be two things: who and what she wants.

—Coco Chanel

When we are born, we come with three things—our bodies, souls, and purposes. Yes, I said purposes. Usually, people only speak of having a single purpose. But we are not one-dimensional beings. We play many roles throughout our lives. Some of those roles are just temporary parts we play. However, some roles have deeper meanings and stretch out for many years, if not an entire lifetime. All of these can be considered purposes.

Are we talking about fate or destiny here? Well, fate is preordained by God, meaning we will experience something regardless of what we do. Destiny still has an element of fate, but we have more choice and influence over events. We have to have these choices and influence because purpose is part of our evolutionary spiritual journey as opposed to our mundane existence in the physical construct. Without our ability to choose or exert influence (and to deal with the consequences of both), we cannot evolve. Therefore, purpose is a product of both fate and destiny.

Though purpose is fundamentally about the lofty aspects of our being, let's not discount the body. On the physical plane, the body and soul can never be separated until after death. While here, they work together, with the soul being superior. The body will grow, constantly changing its shape and size naturally or by modifications we inflict upon it. However, the soul, unlike the body, is fixed and uses the body as a means of transference of purpose from God to a human being. In essence, we are souls with bodies, not the other way around. Without the body, all existence would be mental or spiritual, and God would not have a way to fully experience Himself through us.

Some women seem to know what their purposes are right from the start. However, most of us have to stumble around, and after a few years (perhaps decades) of trial and error, we come to know what we have been brought here to do. Regardless, we can take comfort in knowing that we will not have to fulfill our purposes without some backup from God.

God ultimately owns our souls, and we are stewards. If we attempt to define and execute a purpose based solely on our own understanding, we will be in danger of becoming ego-based and narcissistic. Everything and everyone will appear to be an enemy who is only fit to be obliterated rather than an integral part of some purpose we are called to accomplish.

Though God gave us our missions, He didn't give any of us an owner's manual. We could chalk that up to one of two things. One, God's got a quirky sense of humor. Two, God knew that we would all eventually discover our purposes and somehow meet their demands. I'm inclined to go with number two.

Even when we become conscious enough to know that we have purposes, it may take some time to figure out exactly what they are. After some introspection, we can come to some profound realizations. We may notice that some of the challenges we had in the past, especially the most difficult ones, gave us the experiences and knowledge that can be used for the utilization of our souls. These demanding situations were actually proving grounds to hone our skills and bulk up our spiritual strength.

Being subjected to unpleasant circumstances is a fantastic way to test if we are living the lives God intended for us. They can also be tools used by God to re-direct us to our true purposes if we have detoured. Reflecting on my own life, I now know that one of God's purposes in creating me was so He could experience His own glory through me as I overcame adversity. And though I may have made mistakes, I am trying to better myself daily and constantly strive to be a vehicle for change and positivity. God works through you the same way. So, it is your turn to give Him something awesome to do.

We can only fulfill our God-given purposes by actually living life, not experiencing it through surrogates. Sure, we can acquire intelligent information by reading a book or listening to gurus speak about positive living; but that is only hearsay, and our intellectual understanding of their experience can only take us so far.

This is because there is a difference between having an intellectual understanding about a subject and the application of that same understanding. When it comes to executing our purposes, we must focus on living out the principles of that information and that requires wisdom. Wisdom knows that purpose is not only a noun but also actions that begin with **TO**:

- **TO** build
- **TO** inspire
- **TO** love
- **TO** be graceful
- **TO** be happy

Wisdom is usually obtained and lived when we are doing the work of purposing, especially during times of difficulty or challenge. Though daunting, this aids in our evolutionary growth, which is part of the reason we came here. We must use our struggles or agonizing moments as God's opportunities for us to embody His wisdom rather than lean on wisdom from outside sources. As wisdom-filled women, we'll be able to live out our purposes and accept the peace and grace that gives us.

Boldly embracing our purposes is not done for us alone. Our challenges are tailor-made for us to push past our invisible boundaries. By doing so, we become equipped to help others do the same. Therefore, we must accept all circumstances, no matter what form they take. We go on to keep what is positive and bravely reconstruct the negative.

Ultimately, our souls' collective purposes can be looked upon as a shared calling. You should come to terms with your humanity—its flaws and strengths—as well as others' humanity. Together, moving forward with joy and happiness and not falling into depression over our mistakes or shortcomings, we will be able to celebrate our humanity to the fullest. Optimum awareness of our purposes—our callings—allows us to use all that collected wisdom to impact each other in beneficial ways. That is what all these purposes are about.

UNIVERSAL PURPOSES

Though each of us comes here with an individual set of purposes, there is one that is common to us all—service—whether it be to ourselves or others.

SERVING OURSELVES

Of the two services, service-to-self is the more significant one. We cannot serve (love) anyone else until we serve (love) ourselves. Serving ourselves is an indication that we are dedicated to ensuring our minds, bodies, and souls are in healthy states; basically, we're advocating for our own personal joy and peace at all times.

Serving ourselves is different from being selfish. A selfish woman is only concerned about her own pleasure or profit without any consideration for another. However, serving ourselves stems from the recognition that we have a special place in the world while knowing that we are no better or worse than anyone else. Also, serving is the total acceptance of self and determination to be authentic in the most loving manner.

Okay, accepting and loving oneself seems easy enough. So, why do many of us have such a hard time serving ourselves? Our failure to serve our best interest comes from the belief that we are not worthy of our Creator's love. Even though His love is always accessible, we tend to listen to the ego as it lies, telling us we are damaged.

The scheming ego always brings up the subconscious fears that our faults are beyond forgiveness and God has abandoned us because of it. When we embrace this negativity, we cannot help but to tear ourselves down and live with the constant guilt of never being enough. The ego relishes this because it survives another day to torture our hearts and minds.

However, when you allow yourself to accept God's perfect love, you affirm to your soul that you believe that you are important, that you do matter. In other words, you start to love yourself like God and your soul love you.

As a sign of thankfulness and respect toward God, you do whatever it takes to maintain a healthy life. This self-care is a declarative statement that you recognize your worthiness and expect only the most excellent outcome for yourself without being arrogant. Moreover, your self-care will bolster your development from a mere flesh-and-blood being to a vehicle that God's holiness works through.

Though self-care looks different to everyone, there are some commonalities that can be summed up in the acronym **HER**: **H**uman, **E**ncouragement, and **R**eceiving. Self-care lets us be **human**, giving ourselves mercy during times of weakness. Another common self-care quality is bestowing to ourselves *encouragement* as we endure the rollercoaster ride of life. Also, the gracious *receipt* of others' goodness toward us, without feeling guilty or obligated, is another way to engage in self-care. Using HER, directing self-care toward our minds and bodies subtly impacts everything around us.

With practice, our very presence can become tranquil enough to change the vibration in a room. But until the body catches up with the spiritual vibration, we can take measures to create a wholesome space by reducing lifestyle clutter. We start assessing and becoming choosy about what and how much we take on and consider what is necessary versus unnecessary. Our goal should be the creation of a lighthearted and peaceful space because being in an unhealthy emotional or spiritual place adversely impacts our well-being.

Serving ourselves makes us acutely aware of not only our physical space but also our psychological space. When someone is throwing their emotional baggage at us, these are the times we may have to remind them we are not doormats. Sure, we can help and counsel others, but they have to do the work to sort out their problems. Ultimately, only they can save themselves. Other times, they don't want help; they want to attack. If we find ourselves upset, stressed or befuddled by angry people, those are clues that we are not respecting the sanctity of our psychological space and have somehow allowed negativity to seep into us.

Whenever we're in a discordant state, we should try to immediately disconnect from the stress inducer if we can. If not, instead of letting more tension permeate us, we can mentally disconnect by first counting to ten. That is followed by slow inhalations, making sure the breath goes all the way down to the diaphragm. Try to focus only on the everlasting joy the soul has and fuse with that, even if it is only for a few seconds. Whatever is happening externally does not have to touch us internally. We can only be affected if we bond with the troubling circumstance or person. We really can have a neutral attitude toward external events and people because our external and internal worlds are two separate things.

When you serve yourself, you can more freely express the other universal purpose (serving others). Nourishing yourself is the same as nourishing your connection to your higher power—God—and your soul. Abundant self-love will always keep you satisfied as you bask in the rays of God's unconditional love.

SERVING OTHERS

The next universal purpose is to be connected to our fellow man through service. Relationships are simulations of the nurturing "family" we had when we were still one with the Creator. This drive for connection is ingrained in our souls. Without connections, we can feel lost.

Early on in our development as a species, we acquired a tribal mentality based on our reliance on the small groups we belonged to. This cellular memory stayed with us as we evolved into a modern society. However, we can fight our natural tendency and shy away from connections because of fear. This fear is often based on our inability to be broadminded enough to let different types of people into our personal world. We end up staying with our "own kind" as a precautionary measure. Even worse, the fear of rejection can make us avoid connecting to anyone.

But going against our basic nature and becoming isolated increases stress. Then spiritual longing for connection can turn into physical sickness, increased anxiety due to loneliness, and a sense of despair. Consequently, the stress cycle continues to go around and around because there is no one else around to help get us out of it. However, it should be noted that service is not an excuse for someone to unload their burdens on us. We can lighten each other's load, but we are not to take on pain. Pain that spreads like a virus does no one any good. It dissolves mental clarity and promotes all-around despair. Someone always has to be positive and lucid enough to seek and bring about the change that service engenders.

Women dedicated to service are repositories of empathy and compassion. Again, empathy is not absorbing someone else's pain. It is being able to fully understand another person's plight because we have already experienced the same or can fully imagine what it would be like. Compassion makes us act on the empathy we feel by prompting us to take action.

When we have compassion and empathy, we automatically develop a sensitivity, a certain finesse, about how to deal with other people; we act with diplomacy and genuine concern. Also, compassion and empathy galvanize us to stand up for someone, and intense scrutiny or opposition will not faze us. But not every moment contains a fight. In less intense moments, compassion and empathy can be shown through hospitality. Sometimes a simple invitation to dinner or a day out can make a lonely friend's day.

Tenacity and perseverance are two other virtues that come with the universal purpose of serving others. Tenacity means that we have made a willful decision not to let go of the idea of being of service to others. Perseverance is persistently doing the actual work. Too many times people say they want to be of service but never get around to doing it. On the other hand, some people start a service project but drop it when it demands much time and effort.

However, when we are tenacious and persevering women, we take every opportunity to give to another person. In fact, we may even create outlets for giving if we are innovative enough. We have a no-excuses approach to our service work because we are acutely aware that it is part of the mission.

Confident humility is another aspect of service to others. It is a way of teaching others through example how to live with grace. Confidence in our moral code keeps us focused on the cause and makes sure we're not in it for ego validation. Just because we have confidence in our abilities, we never look down at another person who is in need of our assistance. Instead, confident humility offers loving-kindness. Loving-kindness is more than just being nice. It's the acknowledgment that another person has just as much value as we do.

Ultimately, connecting to our brothers and sisters through service is connecting to God. Service reminds us that we are soul children of God and is one of the great ways we can give our spiritual family the experience of God's love, through us, as we transcend the world.

WHAT IS A TRUE VALUE?

We share universal purposes. But what about those *individual* purposes that are unique to each woman? How do we discover them? A good place to start is with our values.

Many of us define *value* strictly as the monetary cost of something…a typical Western way of looking at the word. Things are seen through a materialistic lens by how many people want the commodity and what price they'll pay to acquire it. Sadly, like material items, people can be bought, too.

There is a more profound definition of "value." This defines value as a principle that is the foundation of our thoughts and deeds and can be life-affirming or denigrating in its orientation. Put in simpler terms, it's the personal philosophy that we live by.

Mundane values are often consequences of upbringing and culture. True values, however, are soul-generated, abstract concepts that are personally important and never hurt or infringe upon another. They are innate and have nothing to do with what our parents, friends, church, or country believe we should want or be. True values stay with us, no matter what we do or do not achieve. These are our unshakable tenets to live by and go along with our purposes.

Before we continue, let me interject some thought-provoking questions: Do you enjoy your occupation, or did you pursue it as a status symbol? Did you buy your car because the women in your social circle drive that type of vehicle, and you wanted to fit in? Is your home a place where you experience peace, or is it something your culture told you that you should want? Are you with your spouse because you adore him or her or because they have superficial value? How much of your life is dedicated to living someone else's?

I ask these material-centric questions because I have come across all types of women from every walk of life. Regardless of their diverse existences, far too often, a common character trait is that many of them use material trappings and other superficial means as barometers for greatness. Misguided values prevent them from finding true happiness, as if they were climbing a mountain with no peak. When we make the acquisition of worldly pleasures and culturally worshipped possessions our main purpose, we tend to lose. There is no way to find happiness in things that need constant replenishment, are forever changing, or will decay. In fact, it may not be the "thing" we actually desire, but the *meaning* of the thing that we crave so much. But we put way too much credence in the symbol rather than the meaning itself. Your answers to those questions were meant to expose if you were doing that.

For us to value something, it has to be meaningful, which usually is an abstraction. The abstraction can be any positive emotion, usually joy or acceptance. Without this key element— meaning—there is no motivation to pursue or invest in any endeavor.

Motivation is acted upon once the meaningful connection is made. When we are madly driven to pursue a goal or a thing, it is a sure bet that some unconscious meaning has intertwined with a surface one. Depending on the thing valued, motivation will be either internal or external.

To help explain the difference between internal and external motivation, let's compare them to being in two geographic locations, the boondocks and the big city. Soul-driven internal motivation is akin to the boondocks. The boondocks are often not easily accessible because of their remote location, just like internal motivation's remote origin is the depths of the soul. This location is also a blessing because that is how the boondocks— just like internal motivation— maintains its most natural state. The boondocks' soothing stillness influences us in such a way that we are inclined to gravitate to it. When we do, we are rewarded with the organic bounty that the boondocks delight in sharing with us, just like the soul does when it gives us our internal motivation.

Internal motivation is not a hard-driving impulse. It can be so soft that it's almost vague. It is more concerned with the process of *being*. To "be" is the reason behind goals that are aligned with what enhances our well-being. When we are *being* something, we usually describe that state in intangible terms such as feelings. The feelings summoned by our internal motivation are ones that cause us to be harmonious and strive to connect with our more sacred values and interests. Moreover, internal motivation causes us to seek out things and activities that we fully savor, basically our God-given impulses and desire to meaningfully connect to others.

However, the big city is like external motivation. It's all about motion, stimulation, and outward excitement. Success in the city depends on whether we decide to work with or compete against other people so that we can acquire and consume. This consumption can be anything…the consumption of food, clothing, relationships, designer handbags, and so on.

Our external motivations are not God-given like internal motivations. Just as big cities are made of concrete, bricks, and steel, external motivations are unnatural. They are fostered as a response to day-to-day living from the time we are born. The truth is that we just can't help developing desires and cravings for pleasures in this world, and there's generally nothing wrong with that.

We must keep in mind that God didn't send us here to be His robots. Even though God tasked us with certain fates, He also gave us free will to explore and achieve some self-directed goals. Going after our personal desires is the process of *doing* and stems from our external motivations. Our doing-ness is based on the hope of gaining material rewards of what we decide to be our mundane life's purpose (money, titles, possessions, fame, etc.). It's the promise of pleasure that make us avoid complacency and make us productive.

In its most positive form, external motivation is positive selfishness. This type of selfishness is a plus because it ensures that we try to provide goodness to ourselves. After all, a healthy protection of self-interest is how we not only survive but also thrive. But this doesn't make external motivation vulgar when compared to internal motivation, as the quest for external as well as internal goals make for a well-rounded human being. In fact, internal motivation often needs to be coupled with an external motivation for a goal to be achieved. For example, a woman who desires to be of service to humanity (internal motivation) needs to raise funds to keep her charity organization going (external motivation). Therefore, she decides to solicit donors and puts together fundraising events to achieve a materialistic goal.

Additionally, external motivation has two passions, harmonious and obsessive. Positive external motivation results in a harmonious passion that integrates easily into our life. Sublime and airy are good ways to describe this passion. However, if we become too spiritualized, we will ignore the concrete work that needs to be done and become lackadaisical. Negative external motivation creates obsessive passion based on instant gratification and egotistical selfishness like the "I'm unhappy so I'm leaving" syndrome. Moreover, obsessive passion causes discord with the soul's integrity and increases the possibility that we will be greedy or fixate on externals.

Successfully managing our passions requires purpose-perspective shifting. Purpose-perspective shifting prevents us from becoming obsessive or lackadaisical as we strive for the equilibrium of harmonious passion.

Whether we step up or try to step down from our purposes, we can never escape God's power or ours. Really, why would we want to? What could be more gracious than accepting our purposes and enjoying the soul power that comes with that? We know deep inside that the longer we wait or try to live according to some other human's standard, the more hardship we will have to complain about. We must make sure we don't end up as the guest of honor at a confetti-strewn pity party. Trust me, I know pity parties feel good, but the complainer will be the only guest because no one else wants to attend.

CULTIVATING YOUR GARDEN

Living out the soul's purposes is similar to tending a prize-winning garden. Both a vibrantly healthy soul that's fulfilling its purposes and a garden's abundant greenery are the optimum outcomes of dedicated effort. However, neither of these favored conditions is guaranteed. Purposes and gardens can fall into disarray and suffer the effects of neglect.

Thriving purposes and bountiful gardens need to be added to at regular intervals. Gardens crave topnotch fertilizer, clean water, and nutritious soil. On the other hand, for our purposes, we need spiritual infusions that can come from religious services, meditative practices, advice from good friends, or communing with nature.

Just like gardens, purposes must undergo symbolic crop rotations and clearings. We do this by gaining new skills and insights. Also, we should try different things and meet new people. This prevents stagnation. And sometimes, we must weed our souls of endeavors that are not productive or have resulted in an infestation of negative outcomes, so they won't take up space and energy.

There is also another way that purposes and gardens are alike. Both of them need boundaries. These lines of demarcation are essentially walls of protection for the soul's purposes. These walls of protection can be breached by the intrusions of external influences that are not in line with the soul's purposes. For example, the walls of vulnerable souls can be scrawled upon by negative comments. In the worst case, boundary walls can be torn down by someone who willfully desires to do us harm.

Our purposes depend on us to stand strong with a determined intention to fortify boundaries. This doesn't mean we are to shut ourselves off from the world, not at all. We can protect our souls and still have a permeable barrier that allows goodness to seep in.

YESTERDAY? TOMORROW? WHY NOT NOW?

How much of our lives do we spend putting off living? What about fretting about things that happened in the past? Why do we constantly fixate on some future event?

Living with purpose is a NOW event. If we are still unsure about our individual purposes, we are to use this present moment to uncover them. We can only live our purposes by claiming ownership of our souls in the present time. Of course, we have to reference the past occasionally and make future plans; that's life. But we can't live any of our purposes if we are stuck in the impossibility called the past or trying to exist in some fantasy called the future.

Fixation on the past can be particularly insidious. But the soul's only interest in the past is to encourage us to take responsibility for our mistakes, learn from them, and make better current choices. But we can't do that until we strip away the ego's ability to keep us constantly focused on the past. The ego wants to give us its purpose by manipulating us into ruminating over past failures and hurts. We lose our sense of self and well-being, donning false beliefs as if they were a heavy, weather-beaten winter coat. This suffocating coat then swallows us up and tricks us into believing that the past is the present and the future.

The only moment we can ever be in is the one we are living right now. Anything other than now is (a) dead and gone and we can do nothing about it or (b) is nothing more than a mere possibility or imaginary future. When we live with purpose, we don't let the concept of time control us. When time (past and future) runs our lives, we live in constant regret of what could have been and worry incessantly about what might happen. Our souls become lifeless because they cannot fix what is gone or control unforeseen circumstances.

But when we opt for living in the present, we immediately start seeing benefits. Our mood uplifts as we begin to notice the delightful occurrences happening all around us. Our creativity soars as serendipitous concepts and ideas start to flow. Our production levels and ability to effectively interact with others increase, too.

Living in the now significantly reduces the chances of running on time-induced autopilot. This gives us the phenomenal ability to make a now-oriented game plan for our purposes. We will make these decisions based on current information instead of past.

Though the past is just a memory, it would be thoughtless to discount it entirely. After all, every past moment has gotten us where we are now, and it is true that we can glean some positive lessons from the past. But the past is only to be referenced briefly for information. Right now, it is up to us to turn our pasts into redemptive stories and change them into powerful purposes that we share with the world. In other words, we are to learn, transform, and move on.

However, constantly living in the moment is nearly impossible to do all the time. In particularly during times of stress, it is easy to find ourselves time traveling and getting caught up in negative emotions. When this occurs, an effective remedy is meditation. Buddhists think of it as a way to calm the monkey mind—restless and uncontrollable thoughts. There are several ways we can meditate effectively and get back on track with our purposes.

Living authentically and focusing more on the journey than the end result is how the true reasons for our purposes reveal themselves. All we have to do is apply the necessary energy and be dedicated. Doing so, we will find that we are enough in this place...that our contributions are worth something. Right now, we should embrace this present moment, accept our purposes, and be one with the world and the Universe.

SOUL AFFIRMATION

I have a purpose and I fully intend to live it out. When I am doing what I have been put here to do, my God-given shine is so bright that the glow makes everyone else's shine turn on, too. That is why I matter. That is why I count. That is why I am important.

CHAPTER 3

OWN YOUR OWN SOUL

The caged bird sings with a fearful trill
of things unknown but longed for still
and his tune is heard on the distant hill
for the caged bird sings of freedom.

—Maya Angelou

I own you. And who am I, you may ask? I am the job you hate but endure because of the money. The bad relationship that brings an endless stream of tears to your eyes. The defeatist reasons you think you can't live out your dreams. The low self-esteem that says you are unworthy of anything good. Basically, I'm anything you've given your power over to. You've never questioned my authority over you; you took it as a given as you bowed down and submitted. I smile because it was so easy to trick you into handing me the control you should have. The truth about me is that I'm a no-thing, a no-body. I'm just a convincing figment of your imagination. If you only knew. Really...who am I, anyway?

That smug monologue is presented to us every day. But like some subconscious dog whistle, we don't hear it with our ears; we hear it with our hearts. This dog whistle is an alert. It sounds off when we can't or refuse to claim our God-gifted souls. Instead, we let external things take the soul's place such as money, lovers, prestige, career, etc. Of course, the loveliness of the soul and the magnificent God that created it are always there. But when we ignore the divine and place our attention on our egos, we *seemingly* relinquish ownership of our lives.

We lose this ownership when we let our negative emotions, brought on by the external world, define us. When this happens anything good we may have thought about ourselves is pushed aside, and the material world fills the void with trash. As we continue to follow the ways of the world, greed, jealousy, rage and other vices start looking like things to aspire to. Our ego-centric minds come to believe this strange existence is the only one and cannot be happy if our warped will is not done.

However, by sharing ownership of our souls with God, we have the beautiful ability to experience the everyday miracles of grace, forgiveness, humility, and love. These higher standards have been instilled in us by our Creator and are common in every human, though sometimes hard to see.

OWNERSHIP OF WHAT, THOUGH?

We all have to contend with taking control of our lives at one time or another. Feeble attempts for control are taken usually when we feel boxed in by some circumstance. However, when we see how much courage and determination is needed to follow through, we fall back on old patterns.

Why do we do that? Maybe it's because we crave ownership over our lives but don't actually know what that means. We can't make a shift toward our full potential until we know what we are taking ownership of and that is:

DEFINING THE SELF

To own our souls is to know who we *really* are. Unfortunately, many external things will seek to define us. We were made into checklists as soon as we were born (gender, race, ethnicity, nationality). On top of that, our families, immediate environments, and greater society tried to mold us into whatever else they thought we should be— projected ideas that had nothing to do with us.

We internalize these expectations and become programmed personalities. We put on our personality costume and act out the part we have been assigned, whether for our good or ill. This will either make us feel like we belong to a loving community or cause us to unwittingly act out negative expectations that have been craftily designed for us. However, because we did not choose the part in the first place, a quiet discontent or fiery rage can take hold, either way.

But what would happen if we asked ourselves, *Who am I? Who do I want to be?* Those two questions can be frightening because, if we answer honestly, those questions dissolve the illusory life we've been living and force us to confront how much ownership of our lives we really *don't* have.

Making the decision to actualize our true selves requires much strength because we may be stripped of our support system in the process. It can be surprising how much the people around us are invested in who they think we are or should be. This is because *they* base what they are on what we are, a strange polarity. If we change, they may be forced to change their ideas of themselves and do away with this polarity (labels/stereotypes/categorizations). Few people want the foundation of their identities disrupted.

How someone else defines their existence has nothing to do with us, though. Our duty is to own a unique identity as the image of the Creator, and we live from that point of view. That viewpoint guides us as we fearlessly live out our own values, no longer allowing the judgments of others to direct and hurt us.

Let's take this moment to look inside ourselves and determine what our "I am" is. This identity is not attached to someone else's identity. It could be who you are, a surgeon, or a mother, or both. You being someone's surgeon or someone's mother is not part of your "I am," although your "I ams" may have been what led to you being drawn to medicine and/or to motherhood.

Perhaps your belief is that a mother is nurturing. Does that mean that since you are a mother you must also be nurturing? It does not. You may be nurturing, or you may not have that quality. Our identities are not defined by our financial status, our education, or jobs, or marital status. Peel back the layers and consider how you want to show up in the world, even if you choose to use your role as a way to start this process. For instance, I want to show up in the world as a good mother. What is a good mother to you? Through drilling down and asking yourself what the essence is of your view of being a good mother or good surgeon, you can uncover your "I ams."

A job does not have power over your "I ams." They are how we want to show up as a conscious human being.

Finding the "I am" that is not attached to being *something* or *someone* in relation to someone else can be hard. But what we are seeking are aspects that are purely us. When we find these aspects, if they are positive, we can and should live them out to the fullest. If they are not to our liking, we have some work to do. Either way, we will finally know what we identify with.

THE CHOICES WE MAKE

We all love the idea of having endless choices. A vast array of choices seems like it would make it easier to choose just the right one, with a beneficial outcome being the final result. If that is the case, why do multiple choices leave us feeling confused about what to do and make us second-guess after a choice is made?

We justify our perplexity by contradicting ourselves by saying we had too many choices. But really, deeper issues are going on like the hidden fear of being wrong and living the consequences of a bad decision. To avoid this, we enlist others in our decision-making process. Not only do we receive help, but we also don't have to take total responsibility for a poor choice. There is someone else to share the blame or assume it all together.

While pushing blame off on someone else may be comforting at first, it eventually destroys self-trust. Gradually, the belief in oneself is eroded, and what is left is fear. Next time, when forced to make a decision on our own, we are crippled with so much doubt that we become paralyzed. Then we have to live with the greater negative consequence of not making any decision at all.

But a woman who owns her choices embraces uncertainty. She understands no one can know all the consequences that any decision will lead to. She bravely trusts herself to make the best choice with the information she has at the time. Though she may ask for others' opinions or expertise, she does not transfer her responsibility to them. She chooses what she believes to be the most constructive action at the time. Whatever the outcome, the expected good or unforeseen misfortune, she owns her choice.

Are most of us going to be expert decision makers, eager to make decisions all the time? The short answer is no. But when the time comes, we have to be determined to overcome our fear of making a mistake and get on with it, because it does not matter how we feel. What matters is we trust that we are capable of taking care of business.

The more choices we make and the more positive outcomes we experience, the more trust we build in ourselves. Even if the outcome was not to our liking, we can see how we took responsibility for it, survived, and went on to make another choice—again, another way to gain trust in ourselves.

OUR FEELINGS AND ACTIONS

How much of our happiness or despair is based on the actions of other people? We gush about people who seem to make us feel joy and bash those who incite unpleasant emotions in us. But it's not external sources that determine our inner state; it's our reactions to them that do.

Emotions are part of the human experience and signals about what we believe to be true. We are responsible for our own thinking patterns, judgments, and actions. Therefore, *our thoughts* about other people's thinking, judgments, and actions have nothing to do with them.

When we don't own our emotions and feelings, we give others the ability to manipulate our lives. If they make us feel good, we don't mind giving up ownership and handing over our minds. However, if what they are doing results in pain, we relinquish our power even more by blaming them for our sad state. In turn, we feel justified in returning their attack with attack or we use our sense of powerlessness to support our lack of determination to change the situation.

As we project our negative feelings on to another person, we turn sour. Our minds spiral downwards as we lose control. Irksome thoughts, of how things would have been better if the other person took other actions, create chaos in our spirits.

The flip side is that other people may blame us for their responses. We are not responsible for the feelings of other adults. However, this does *not* relieve us of personal responsibility regarding how we treat others. After all, there is always a karmic effect resulting from our behaviors.

However, right now, we are more interested in our own feelings and how ownership enables us to choose our response to any given stimuli. Ownership will let us correctly identify the issues surrounding a conflict instead of becoming part of the problem. In the process, the ego's obnoxious voice is quieted, and the calming whisper of the soul can be heard.

When we own our feelings, we also own our actions. Actions are the physical responses to our feelings as we accept our part in every situation. Taking action is re-creating ourselves and situations into more positive forms. For example, we may have to be the peacemaker, despite the ego telling us to do the opposite. Sometimes we will just have to walk away from the conflict instead of engaging in it. Still, there may be times when seeking restitution is proper, but we can see justice served without being destructively emotional. No matter what course of action is appropriate, being responsible for our actions will require strength because acting out is so much easier to do.

We just have to remember that we are in charge of our joy despite what anyone else is doing. Relying on our own minds, guided by God, we will be able to transcend the ego's perceptions and deal with all situations with grace. Simply put, if we do not like something, we can either accept it or change it, and there will no longer be a need to rely on external sources to buoy our spirits or validate our existences. Genuine happiness springs from that.

Owning our choices, feelings, and actions is the same thing as becoming a leader. Taking leadership of our lives allows us to release blame. We have the power to overcome difficult circumstances without putting responsibility on someone else. We'll have no problem accepting that life is not going to just give us what we want, and we give up the expectation that externals are supposed to offer us comfort. Instead, our fulfillment comes from within.

BREAK THE BOX OFFICE

Taking ownership of our lives is like being in a really good movie. We become the multi-dimensional central character who desires to break free of some constraint at the story's beginning. As our stories unfold, we meet friends and foes, encounter doubt and failure, and make small steps toward progress by overcoming risk aversion. With dedication, we achieve our goal of self-actualization by the end of the movie.

Joseph Campbell, an American writer and mythology enthusiast, recognized this particular structure inserted into storytelling calling it the hero's journey. This journey is undertaken by an often-reluctant hero who has to go out into the world, faces tremendous obstacles, and return home with a bounty that he shares with his family or community.

Popular movies, books, and television shows use some form of the hero-journey structure almost exclusively. The reason why this mythological pattern is so popular in storytelling is because it tends to reflect how the average person achieves goals.

Just like a main character, when we decide to own our lives, we usually have to make the difficult transition from being passive in an area to dynamic. Taking the reins of power is often a scary and troublesome task. Let's be honest: it is so much easier to kick back and let someone else handle things and remain unburdened by responsibility. But our souls fight that notion. They know we aren't here to simply follow others' directives.

To prevent stagnancy, souls will gently nudge us towards independence by putting us in "soft" conflict situations or giving us internal dissatisfaction. However, if we are stubborn or too frightened to take control, our souls will bring forth more charged situations to push us to change.

It is obviously best to avoid a personal "order out of chaos" situation. Before that happens, we can take the initiative to find out what areas we need to take ownership of. There is a pattern in storytelling, a certain sequence of events. Maybe that pattern of storytelling is part of the collective unconsciousness, or the way the human mind is wired to process information. But whenever we seek to obtain self-governance or make choices in a particular area of our lives, the process tends to conform to the pattern of the hero's journey. When we uncover the areas of our lives that we want to change, we can use *our interpretation* of a hero's transformation to mold ourselves into sovereign women:

STAGE ONE: THE CURRENT SITUATION

This is our world before we make changes. Sometimes we don't even know a change needs to be made. Regarding ownership, someone or some situation is calling the shots for us. We may not like it, but we haven't made an effort to change, usually because we are receiving some sort of safety or reward by subduing our power.

STAGE TWO: THE UNSETTLING

A disruptive event comes along that threatens to jeopardize the safety or reward we receive because we relinquished our ownership. We become painfully aware that we will have to become the ruler of some area of our lives but recognize that won't be easy to do.

STAGE THREE: THE SHAKEUP

We notice how stagnant or destructive our lives are. However, it has been so comforting to let someone else own a part of us. Though we may want to take command, inner fears and insecurities make us back down. Some decide to just keep things the way they are. They try to live the same old way but now have doubts that shake them up. Others start their transition, but the shakeup is not enough to make them fully commit.

STAGE FOUR: MEETING A MENTOR

A mentor arrives to motivate us to change. The mentor can come in any form such as an inner voice. A mentor can also be a person such as an intimate friend who has taken full control of her life and is an inspiration, or it can be a life coach. Sometimes it is just a wise stranger who offers much needed insight.

STAGE FIVE: THE "OH S***" MOMENT

Up until this moment, if we aren't fully committed to our goal, we can go back to our old situation. However, something happens to us, often something unpleasant. That event makes us realize that we can't stay at the level we're at; we have to make a move. Sometimes we are forced to do so. The decision to take action happens at this point. This is what really gets the "story" going. A decision to take ownership is made. Though this is unfamiliar territory, undaunted, we go forward.

STAGE SIX: WHO DO YOU TRUST?

Challenges will test how much faith we really have. Other people stand in our way or sabotage our efforts. But there are still people we can trust, and they will offer support in whatever way we need it. We may even be surprised at who our allies and enemies reveal themselves to be.

STAGE SEVEN: THE BOOGIE MAN

This is actually the point where we confront our greatest hidden fears. Don't take this step lightly; it is a struggle. As we move closer to total self-ownership, the tests will get harder. We may even have more failures than successes. However, the victories that we achieve will keep us going.

STAGE EIGHT: REBIRTH

The transformation process becomes more intense. We'll be in some circumstance where the only way we can move forward is to deny our "old" self so that a new self can be born. This can only be done by utilizing the skills we learned during our journey. As we do this, we mentally (and sometimes physically) transform into another person by annihilating self-defeating thoughts.

STAGE NINE: THE BOUNTY

We are no longer the same person we were at the beginning and have obtained the goal. We own ourselves. Time to celebrate!

STAGE TEN: GOTTA SHARE

We discover something about ownership—that whenever we take charge of some part of our life, we affect other people. If we had self-centered interests, we might find this daunting. That is totally understandable; we just want to enjoy our reward and not be concerned about the resonating effects. But the true power of ownership is that it isn't only for us but for others as well. We now have responsibilities. And we have to master our new-found abilities with the intent of sharing.

STAGE ELEVEN: TRAVELING THE PATH BACK HOME

It takes time for us to learn how to become masters. We will seem to be doing well, until ghosts of our past life show up to demolish the areas that we claimed ownership over. This is our last stand. Whether the ghosts are external or internal, we must vanquish them, or they will certainly vanquish us. At some point, it may seem like the ghosts have destroyed and taken us back to hell, but somehow we rise from the dead. Any inner conflict we have, we master it.

STAGE TWELVE: ARRIVING HOME

Mastery is a purification process. It doesn't take too long for anyone to see that we are strong and own our lives. We are inspirations to other women who find themselves in the same state that we were in at the beginning of our journey.

STEPPING UP TO OWNERSHIP

Becoming brave enough to claim ownership over our lives is not an easy task. Most of us have to fight a lifetime of programming that is diametrically opposed to the freedom that self-control brings. The journey toward ownership can be strenuous and exhausting; however, there are easily accessible ways to manage the stress:

MAKE DECISIONS

We are constantly deciding between living someone else's life and authentically living our own. Giving up authenticity is a sure sign that we are submitting to someone else's decision making. To overcome this, throughout the day, we should silence our minds for a few moments and listen to our hearts. They will remind us of who we really are. After carefully listening, we accept the messages. Then we use them to love ourselves more by living authentically and bravely making decisions.

ADOPT NEW THOUGHTS

Once we have made a choice to own our decisions, we'll be infused with new thoughts about ourselves and ways to relate to the world. This is a gradual process because, initially, the mind will reject what it doesn't believe. We start by professing positive thoughts we already believe about ourselves. We can also use affirmations such as "I'm safe. I'm worthy. I'm loved." These affirmations can prime us to accept beneficial outcomes and give us more self-confidence to make better decisions in the future.

BE SPECIAL

Each one of us really is special. We have unique talents and skills, and we already use them to some degree, even though we may not be aware of it. To uncover our gifts, nightly, we can write down three positive things we did that day. It doesn't matter how insignificant we think it was. The piece of paper will reveal how we actually use our hidden skills and talents. We should consider whatever good we did to be a miracle because we added some much-needed goodness into the universe. In fact, we can call those nightly write-ups our Miracle Journals. We can refer to these miracles whenever we need to be reminded of how good we are.

EMBRACE DUALITY

We can be strong yet tender and vulnerable. Too much strength makes us hard like rocks. Conversely, too much softness turns us into weaklings. Mastering both sides is necessary for ownership. Any area we command requires us to adapt by using a well-rounded personality. The strong woman part of us makes sure we maintain authority. Our yielding side allows us to relax or ask for help, which are also signs of strength.

LEARNING CURVE

We are born clean slates to be written upon by our experiences. A learning curve automatically exists for everything we do, including taking ownership of our lives. It is up to us whether or not we will be happy or sad learners.

If we decide to be sad-learners, we act out in different ways. First, we can renounce the power of ownership. When lessons present themselves, we feel victimized and can't see the blessing, let alone learn from it. We then go through life experiencing the same problems and quit when adversity strikes as we wonder why everything has to be so hard, so caught up in judging and dwelling. In the tumult, as sad learners, we become cracked. At first, the cracks can be fixed; however, they go on to be unrepairable due to our lack of ownership.

Next, our sad-learner perspective sees danger everywhere. We become engulfed by our fight-or-flight mentalities instead of allowing challenges to be opportunities to grow within ourselves. Fixed in our limiting beliefs, we let circumstances create our lives. Desperation eventually gets the best of us. We use avoidance just to catch a break from the pain and give our control over to others.

Handing over ownership is not a passive activity but a powerful free will decision.

As we allow others to be our saviors, we willfully fail to learn another lesson about ownership—the one about having a voice. We accept their opinions about who we are, especially when they tell us we aren't good enough. We believe the false conditioning that those most dear to us give, and our self-image becomes whatever they decide. Manipulative family members, abusive spouses, and unreliable friends can have the final say-so. Sad learners also hand over their free will to the voice of the past. The past mocks us by saying what happened is what defines us, and we can't be saved. Experiences become antagonistic ghosts that howl in the present. They haunt like bad spirits possessing the soul.

Also, in sad-learner mode, we operate through pride. Our haughtiness comes when we actually do take ownership and think that means being right all the time or above someone else. We become demanding, acting like spoiled children, stomping our feet. We bully up on others mentally, emotionally, and sometimes physically just to get our way. But as we fight others to get our desires met, we make those desires harder to obtain because others meet our aggression with aggression and block them.

But our aim is to be happy learners. As happy learners, we see all circumstances as a chance to grow. We understand that growth comes from the adversity built into the experience of being human. Instead of lamenting the prospect of constant challenges, we bravely accept them. After the battles have been fought, we may come out scarred, but we look at those marks as life tattoos that prove we have been there, done that, and survived. All that heartache only made it possible for us to feel bliss more intensely.

Forever facing forward, as happy learners, we accept the growing pains that accompany the accumulation of knowledge. Sometimes that pain can seem unbearable when we're going through it. But somehow, we'll come to remember that nothing lasts forever, including pain. We will manage to stumble to our feet and stand tall again. The wind at our backs will push us along to the next lesson, a lesson that will be there for a reason.

Also, we have a chance to be thrilled about the prospect of living life on our own terms. It's wonderful that we can dedicate every minute of our precious lives to the pursuit of being positive, learning to trust the process, and becoming wise. Mistakes are inevitable, but we still hold a vision of a better tomorrow.

One of a happy learner's greatest lessons is that we cannot control everything. We have been given stewardship over certain areas, and it is up to us to learn and accept what they are. There will be times when we have to relinquish control over what does not belong to us and great faith may be required to do so. But we know that releasing the idea of certainty can sometimes be the only way some crises can be dealt with. We take responsibility for what we can and should be doing. Regarding everything else, let it go and give it to God.

WHO YOU CALLING A B#&%*?!

Claiming ownership sometimes calls for us to summon our inner bitch. The inner bitch is a God-given resource that is always there to help and give us strength. She usually shows up when we have become lax in maintaining the walls of protection for our souls.

As a personalized warrior, she is the one who vigilantly patrols the wall of protection's boundaries, keeping them secure. Also, the inner bitch is the one who faces unpleasant tasks, and she gives the courage to confidently deal with difficult people. The inner bitch can do this because she knows how to take initiative and keep self-confidence stoked. Basically, the inner bitch does not allow anyone to walk over you.

However, we have to know how to handle the inner bitch when she shows up. She can be difficult because we may not know how to use her potent energy, and some women are afraid of her power. As a result, they may actually become weaker in their inner bitch's presence rather than strengthened.

Other women act like volcanoes when they embrace the inner bitch. Those particular women may have been suppressing their power for so long that the internal pressure has reached a critical point. When they become angry, their inner bitch explodes at whoever is around, often with venomous words and rage in a disproportionate amount to what the situation calls for. PMS or menopause is often blamed, but those unfortunate actions usually have more to do with feeling powerlessness and exhaustive frustration rather than hormones.

Nuclear reactions or passive defeatism can be avoided altogether if we take the time to strengthen our walls of protection in the first place. Anger, hostility, and fear may allow for the occasional crossing of the wall of protection's threshold. But when the wall has been properly maintained, these uncommon occurrences can be counter-measured. Responses will be appropriate, and our souls will still be owned by us.

Taking ownership means taking control of our lives. We really can handle whatever comes along, and even if we don't know how to deal with it straightaway, we will figure it out.

PENETRABLE FOG

Taking ownership is like stepping into a dense fog bank. Not being able to see through it offers no comfort, but there is a prize waiting on the other side. Once you accept that you must take control and own the situation, you become an empowered woman.

Pushing fears aside, you step into the foggy cloud. Though others may try to pull you back from the ominous mist, you break away with the courage to go your own way, being true to yourself. As you make your way through the unknown, you'll vanquish whatever is hidden in there.

When you emerge from the fog, you'll have learned to embrace what made you ache, forced you to change, and inspired you to move ahead in the first place. There is no need for the fog to disappear. You just have to keep telling yourself, "I'm incredible enough to go through it."

SOUL AFFIRMATION

I own my successes.
I own my failures.
I own my learning.
I own my forgetting.
I own my choices.
I own my rejections.

But no matter what, whether I have
laughter or tears, I will always own
everything that is me.

CHAPTER 4

SOUL WARRIOR

Praying is the time to ask
and meditating is the time to listen.

—Gabrielle Bernstein

There's no doubt about it…this world contains so many attractions—things like laughter, beauty, sensual pleasure, and above everything else, love. We can't help but to be in awe of the everyday brilliance or resplendence we encounter.

However, as we look at the world's projection screen of loveliness, every so often we can catch glimpses of distorted images. We start to see more confusion and madness, which makes us wonder what kind of world we really live in. As we witness more mayhem in our lives or the lives of others, we may even start to question God. After all, why would a triple-omni-God (omnipresent, omnipotent, and omniscient) create such a beautiful monstrosity called *the world?*

As soul women, we have to understand what this plane of existence really is. No one can argue that "something" had to create it, for it exists. It is not a random configuration of particles, elements, and minerals. Therefore, our world has to have a purpose.

I am not going to sugarcoat this because doing so will not help. The world is a place of warfare. But this is not just any kind of warfare…it is spiritual warfare. At some particular point in space and time, our Father had a plan for us. It was for mankind to have everlasting life. We agreed to come here and fulfill His purpose. But everlasting life is not given to incredibly flawed beings. We must be tested and purified.

This world is the proving ground for that process. Our births placed us directly into this battlefield. We all arrived with specific opponents and challenges to overcome, and some of us have more formidable ones than others. That does not mean that we are innately "evil" and being punished if we are currently facing harsher obstacles than others. It may mean that we are just braver.

Because God is always in control, He makes sure that the world-wide battle does not get out of control. Sure, it seems like the entire world is just a globe of chaos at times, but somewhere balance is being maintained.

As we continue journeying forth, we will meet sets of challenges. Someone may be nudged to be the catalyst for one of our life lessons or purposes. Other times, we will be "inspired" to be the unpleasant catalyst for another. This in no way negates anyone's responsibility.

The-devil-made-me-do-it excuse is not legitimate. The nudges for humans to be and act as negative catalysts are in actuality tests, too. This has to do with the true purpose of free will. We have free will to decide what we will do within a field of choices. The way everything plays out is up to us.

For both the put-upon and the aggressor, the spiritual war revolves around what choices the individuals make. See, those nudges that urge us to veer toward the negative *do not* come directly from God. They come from powers beyond our comprehension, though they are lower than God. Moreover, God did not cause someone to be diseased, impoverished or murdered. These are just the manifestations of endless possibilities in this world. The reality is that pain is inevitable; suffering is not. Suffering is a choice based on how we decide to deal with pain.

Regardless of our particular challenges, we are called upon to be soul warriors. Our attitudes determine our approach. As we engage in spiritual warfare, we will have to decide whether we are happy learners or victims. Of course, we want to be happy learners. When we adopt the attitude that this world is a learning device for the soul, we will be empowered and able to overcome our emotional and spiritual weaknesses.

A true spiritual war will not be sparked by transitory problems, though. We will know a spiritual war from a mundane problem by its intensity and duration. For example, a drug addiction will cause a spiritual war whereas a having a bad reaction to a drug is a mundane problem. That bad reaction will pass but a drug addiction will threaten your "I ams" for the rest of your life. During a spiritual war, some outside force (human or illness or something else) will present some form of anti-goodness. This foe oftentimes will activate one of our sore spots. Also, it may cause us to experience a profound sense of loss and incredible pain of some kind. If left unchecked, it will most likely overwhelm our minds, and its effects will linger for some time.

To win the war, we can't allow ourselves to stay in a place of pronounced misery. We must come to the realization that our battles are not with circumstances or people; the battles are with ourselves. No matter what is happening, we are really battling our own insecurity, fear, and guilt. These are signs that we have handed over our internal power to something or someone else, and we forgot how great we are. Sometimes it may take anger to help us remember.

Anger is not necessarily something we have to take into battle all the time because not every situation warrants it. However, we may need a proper motivating force to fire us up enough to do battle to begin with. Righteous anger is dynamic when it is united with intelligence and action. This kind of anger is what gets us off our bums and makes us advocate for ourselves and others. But be careful. If we *think* our foes are too powerful, our initial fiery anger alone may not be enough and gets extinguished, and we may decide to give up straightaway.

There is another caveat that comes with anger. Even though anger can be productive at first, our emotional state should not remain there. If we stay in a place of anger, it will turn into rage. Then it is just a matter of time before we implode on ourselves. Rage is totally destructive (seeks to harm) and makes us run on a hamster wheel of negative emotion; we just fester in fury.

So, if staying angry is dangerous and desire can wane, how do we find the unblinking motivation to engage in spiritual warfare? The answer is not complicated. To arouse the energy to go to battle and stay there, something has to be at stake. That means that if we do not conquer the challenge, we or someone we care about will endure some sort of *perceived* suffering or spiritual death.

If we are still unsure about how to raise the energy to go into spiritual battle, we can ask ourselves three questions:

What have I allowed this circumstance or person to take from me? Think in terms of spiritual and emotional assets, not physical ones.

What dreadful things am I doing to others or letting someone do to me with regards to this situation? It is important not to go into blame mode here. This is not the time for the projection of guilt or internalizing shame. You are just getting an honest assessment of what is going on.

How am I compromising myself right now? Look to see if you have turned your back on your value system or are violating your moral code just so you can deal with a particular person or circumstance.

As spiritual warriors, we can't hole up in our safe spaces. We have to get out there, despite the war. Battling on, it's guaranteed there will be a time when we will want to lash out at God and scream, "Why?" But dear ones, even if He gave us all the answers, we probably still could not comprehend them anyway. Instead of waiting to be coddled, we should accept the challenge and don our spiritual armor.

Our spiritual armor will be steeled by decisions: The decision to be proactive, refusing to be led by circumstances. The decision to use the power of faith instead of succumbing to despair. The decision to lead others by example by showing them that the power of grace can overcome negativity. The decision not to peel off our armors during times of physical or emotional pain.

The armor-building process prepares us for whatever circumstances life brings. The process need not be intimidating. After making the aforementioned decisions, it can be done gradually. This is a benefit because long-term change is usually permanent. But whether our armor is built over time or through an emergency that requires a quantum leap, just remember, you'll make it through.

PRAYER WARRIOR

At the outset of any spiritual battle, we will pick a side, whether we are consciously aware of what is going on or not—between God and an enemy opposed to goodness. It doesn't matter if this enemy is a human being, a circumstance, or an environment. The enemy's relentless impact will be the same.

If we are consciously aware, our active choices determine which side we are placed on. However, if we are running on automatic pilot and blindly reacting to the hostile force, we will be placed on the enemy's team by default.

Moreover, we may be tempted to think it's easier to simply succumb to the effects of the enemy. Though the power of the enemy is not insurmountable, it can appear to be unusually robust and maybe unbeatable. We may be tempted to think that the enemy's team is the place to be. But before we reach the event horizon of some bad decision, we should call upon the power of prayer.

A soul warrior is simultaneously a prayer warrior. A prayer warrior is a soldier whose mission is to make sure our General's (God/Higher Power) purposes for us are fulfilled. Prayer warrior's fight for that destiny and are willing to give up everything for the charge.

Prayer is an "atomic" power. Although it is a God-given gift, we must not wield this power lightly. As prayer warriors, we respect the power of prayer because of its potency. Prayer can be likened to surging energy and responds to the emotion and intention of its user. Truly, prayer can alter things for the better if performed by a wise person (positive prayer) and can increase adversity when used by a selfish person (negative prayer). The latter form of prayer is inverse prayer, meaning that it is contrary to the creative will of God. Either way, prayer changes things.

Of course, we are aiming for positive prayer. Positive prayer is not vague; it is specific. Generally, it is performed by a prayer warrior who shows that she has some understanding of the root problem. If she does not know what the root of the issue is, she never hesitates to ask God for clarity. Her positive prayers help to alleviate stress and worry during times of uncertainty, calm the spirit, and offer a chance to unplug from distressing circumstances. Her faith deepens as she is open to receiving what she hopes for, but she is also willing to accept whatever the outcome is.

As the answered prayer makes its way to the prayer warrior, there may still be difficulties to contend with, and the prayer warrior asks how she should handle them. Then she quiets her mind to hear or feel the answer. Any prayer warrior should take heed not to mistake the ego's voice for God's or else failure in the spiritual battle is the result. When we discern the difference between our ego and God, and decide to follow the right path, God will turn us into spiritual weapons experts. Aside from prayer, our arsenals will consist of:

BRAVERY

Bravery is not the absence of fear. It is the ability to move forward in spite of fear and challenge. Prayer warriors keep praying, especially when it appears that those prayers are not making any sort of difference. Bravery makes a prayer warrior hold on, refusing to submit to the pain threatening to overtake her. She tightens the laces on her spiritual combat boots, going deeper into her prayers until a breakthrough occurs.

STRENGTH

Awareness of the true problem and acceptance of its existence can be difficult for some; they do not believe they have the necessary strength to overcome it. However, the spiritual enemy rarely slinks away and therefore has to be faced. Those who step into battle, despite daunting odds, are often given strength. Strength is not only confined to the physical body. Strength is in the mind and spirit as well. Prayer warriors need this vigor to bear the metaphorical and sometimes real blows the enemy delivers.

INTELLIGENCE

Pure emotionalism in a spiritual war can cause defeat. However, the ability to read emotion, combined with rational intelligence, is a spiritual weapon that allows us to uncover and understand the truth about the trial we are going through, especially if there is a pronounced human factor involved. Also, intelligence gives us problem-solving ability by utilizing critical thinking and abstract creativity.

DOMINANCE

We realize that we're not helpless and don't have to be obedient to anyone or anything that doesn't care about our best interest. We are in charge. We handle the spiritual war; it will not handle us. Though God has given us this weapon, we must want to take control and the responsibility that comes with it.

Even when we utilize our spiritual weapons, some wars can be excruciatingly long and frightfully difficult. Because of many detours, even a prayer warrior's spiritual armored tank can run out of gas. The uncommitted warrior will probably decide to just give up and remain stranded in the tank, with the enemy's brigade swiftly approaching. However, a prayer warrior will steel up her faith and pray fervently. She knows that eventually God's mobile gas truck will arrive and fill her tank back up. As the spiritual gas fills the tank, the prayer warrior is renewed. She can rush back into combat, annihilating every obstacle in her path. That is how prayer warriors eventually claim bold victories.

CONFLICT

Conflict is where the soul warrior gets into the nitty-gritty of the mission. As much as we wish it wasn't true, the reality is that it's impossible for a soul warrior to live in this world and not experience some conflict due to the destiny they are to fulfill. This destiny drives the warrior's desires and values and often opposes others' desires and values, resulting in conflict of interests.

We all jockey to see who will have their desires met and whose values will dominate, causing us to go into survival mode. Scarcity and blame blind our true vision. However, it's the choices (determined by their mindset) that a soul warrior makes that determines whether or not conflict is constructive or destructive.

The brashest of us have absolutely no fear of conflict. But some soul warriors of this type seek out destructive or nonproductive conflict. Though their initial impulse may be positive, impudent soul warriors may go headlong into battle and unintentionally become overbearing and self-serving because they are led by their egos. For them, compromise or helping to implement someone else's vision seems like failure. A good outcome for them is to get everything they want, while someone else gets nothing. The way this selfishness is accomplished is by being pushy, argumentative, bullying, and through alienation. These actions can have a draining effect on those around them, leaving others resentful or angry and wanting to push back. As a result, instead of furthering their agenda, these audacious warriors alienate potential allies and accomplish nothing.

Brave soul warriors, on the other hand, use conflict constructively. For them, conflict resolution starts with the self, and they do the work of healing their own inner conflict. After they stabilize themselves, they desire to share that stability with others; but they are keenly aware that even under the best of circumstances, conflict with others may turn sour and sometimes contentious. Yet they are undeterred because they are success-oriented and see present circumstances as temporary hurdles toward progress. In that way, conflict is a precursor to problem resolution, and these soul warriors optimally utilize it as they put a give-and-take strategy in place.

Both groups (constructive and destructive) at least try to have some forward motion when it comes to conflict, whether their motives be altruistic or selfish. However, some people do whatever they can to sidestep any and all conflict. These reluctant soul warriors are avoiders. They should not simply be mistaken for nice people, for even nice people still use conflict in their own way to achieve their goals.

Avoiders have a tendency to believe the very nature of conflict is negative. After all, most psychologically-grounded soul warriors do not actively seek destructive conflict; peacefulness is a more desirous state of being. But even the most peace-loving soul warrior recognizes that conflict breaks us out of ruts, brings serious problems to the fore and makes it possible to solve them, helps us become more creative, and results in better communication. However, conflict avoiders fear having to face the consequences of expressing what they want or revealing feelings like anger or mistrust. In fact, conflict avoiders may actually feel guilty or anxious when they do. So instead of them using the power of their inner soul warrior, they ignore her believing their silence is safer than utilizing their free will and voice. They also wrongly believe that keeping the peace at the expense of the truth or growth is beneficial. However, the opposite is often the case. The avoider may be at risk for bullying, becoming an enabler, or engaging in martyrdom.

As the repressed soul warrior elects to serve others' needs at the expense of her own, coupled with denial, lowered self-esteem may occur. The resultant inertia guarantees that the warrior experiences no mental or spiritual growth and is cast as a background character in someone else's story. Other times, she can become passive-aggressive as she covertly takes out her festering anger on others because her needs are not being met. Ironically, her needs are not met because she never voiced them directly. Her passive-aggressiveness then comes out through complaining behind someone's back, failing to follow-through with her part of others' plans, or ruminating and holding grudges silently in her heart.

But when it comes to disagreement, conflict avoiders usually try to avoid discord with the ones they love and value the most. When avoiders skirt conflict at home, they may start to lack integrity and through their actions unwittingly say that the issue before them is not that important. Consequently, the home falls apart.

Though it is frightening and uncomfortable, engaging in growth-causing conflict is a clear demonstration that our relationships are important and a profound expression of willingness to evolve. Conversely, the extremes of conflict—avoidance and constant fighting—are main contributors to relationship break-down, no matter what form that relationship may take. For conflict to have a successful outcome, all parties must know that conflict resolution is a balancing act between wants, needs, and compromise.

The handling of conflict can come about in a variety of ways depending on the context of the relationship. Both sides should be expected to behave in a mature manner and accountable for their own behavior. Also, they should agree upon an overall goal and have a willingness to achieve it. As arguments are put forth, everyone should be objective, open to listening to someone else's point of view, and compromise when necessary.

If the conflict happens to be personal, neither person should give judging opinions, but they should speak about how they feel. For example, phrases like "I feel like…" or "I am noticing…" could be used. Also, the focus should be on the current conflict rather than past issues unrelated to what is happening right now.

Regardless of the type of conflict, emotional triggers may be activated. Conflict can make us feel threatened by touching on our past pain. But we should do our best to separate the present conflict from a trigger by seeing them as two different events.

As we deal with conflict, we feel less stress, become stronger, and actually accomplish goals and ambitions. We no longer have to be afraid of confrontation, and problems will be resolved instead of being brushed off. In the end, no matter the environment or how uncomfortable the process is, everyone eventually benefits from conflict resolution.

PEACEKEEPING MISSION

Sometimes soul warriors have to engage in conflict on someone else's behalf. During these times, the soul warrior will give support and strength to others who need boosts. The stakes can be high because the consequences are multiplied by however many people are involved in the situation.

But as soul warriors, we are duly prepared since our unique struggles equipped us with skills, resources, and insights that can benefit others. We can feel confident enough to stand side-by-side with other "soldiers" during their battles by offering up powerful prayers, giving desperately needed financial help, or simply propping them up as they go through their storms.

Because nothing lasts forever, a break from spiritual combat comes eventually, and we and our fellow soul warriors can take breaks. Although this is a feel-good time, there is still work to be done through maintenance.

The maintenance phase is protecting and actively preserving— to the best of our ability—the goodness created from the soul battle you endured with another warrior. But we are realists and know that it is all too easy to slip back into old patterns. This is why mainte-nance also allows for the inevitable day when we or someone else, once again, needs the help of another soul warrior. Ah, the ebb and flow of life never ceases.

Recognize that progress born out of joint endeavors requires peace. Think of peace as cooperation between higher minds that needs to be maintained, similar to the peacekeeping efforts of the military or allied governments. In this regard, try to imagine our-selves as U.N. peacekeepers by using their three basic principles.

The first principle is that everyone involved in the situation must commit to idea of peace. The ultimate purpose of being a soul war-rior is personal and mutual peace. If the other party involved doesn't have the same goal, no matter what a soul warrior does, the result will always end up in war. As soul warriors, we must make the distinction between our allies and those who will be at cross-purposes with us. After all, only the willing can be helped.

The second principle is impartiality. We must develop the ability to see all sides of a situation when it comes to helping people and maintaining peace. Our neutrality must be intellectually informed yet intuitive. However, being impartial does not mean being blind. Bad behavior must be called out and dealt with swiftly yet fairly.

Finally, the third principle is to avoid the use of unnecessary force. There is never a need to use emotional violence (guilt) or bully tactics to make anyone accept help or preserve goodness they received after our intervention. This goes back to the first principle that everyone should commit to a peaceful outcome right from the start. Moreover, though we don't help other people for kudos, they should be grateful for the help they've received and want to secure it.

But we must keep in mind that we are not the commander of other people's lives; it is up to them to work with or against us. There is never a need to force someone to accept our help or at least be appreciative of it. If they go against our expectations, we may be tempted to lash out. However, soul warriors know that they are not here to vengefully punish anyone for their so-called infractions.

However, egotistical people who constantly overstep polite boundaries don't care about meeting expectations. They're operating from faulty ideas when they push and use us, and this naturally sparks cause and effect. Therefore, we have the absolute right to stand up and protect our spaces or someone else's. When doing so, we must be elegant and graceful, as humanly possible, with the karma we deliver, though. Refuse to be jaded and continue to soldier on for others. That's the soul warrior's way.

HUMBLE WARRIOR

We've all likely had our share of formidable foes and clawed our way through some pretty arduous battles. The best artillery would have been used against us and somehow, we still emerged victorious. Yes, that is all that awesome-ness in us. However, before we start popping champagne bottles, words of caution must be offered.

A soul warrior can become so enamored by her own success that she can start to mistake arrogance for confidence. The primary problem with this arrogance (pride) is that it causes a soul warrior to put her own needs and specialness above God's plan. And even though the soul warrior might have some initial success, she may end up failing at some point because the assignments God gives each one of us cannot be amended by mere human beings; however, the prideful refuse to acknowledge that.

Instead of accepting her soldier-hood in the spiritual war with a humble heart, pride can make a soul warrior look upon her duty with contempt. Pride makes soul warriors think, *I know what should happen, and I'm going to bend reality to my will. I handled things before, and I didn't even need God. Now that I think about it, since I'm such a good person, this circumstance shouldn't even be happening to me. How dare God allow this to go on!*

Inflated self-worth also makes a soul warrior extremely self-centered. A prideful warrior spends an inordinate amount of time protecting her ego-image rather than focusing on the greater good.

Also, sometimes in a spiritual war that involves many people, the prideful forget who the enemy is and become antagonistic towards their fellow soldiers for a myriad of reasons—pettiness, jealousy, power struggles, etcetera. This defensive stance drains energy away from the spiritual war at hand. Instead of standing strong together, the group becomes splintered as they set their attention on inconsequential side fights.

Unfortunately, sometimes in our culture, the most arrogant and pushy among us are often celebrated and used as examples of how to be successful. Rudeness and self-importance are portrayed as desirable traits. Humbleness, on the other hand, is often characterized as a defect or weakness. When it comes to media propaganda and dog-eat-dog societal norms, humble people are perceived as timid, lacking willpower, and easy to force to submit. Two of the most damaging ideas about humbleness are that it is a degrading personality trait and that it is one of the quickest ways to get *left behind* in life.

Ironically, humbleness is a sign of an ultimate soul warrior. The beauty of a humble warrior's strength comes from the fact that she has nothing to prove. She aims at fulfilling her own potential and not at anyone else's expense. Moreover, a soul warrior's humbleness is based on her commitment to being selfless—she thinks of her "self" less.

That selflessness gives the humble warrior the ability to be team-oriented, constantly striving for optimistic cooperation, because she feels that we are all in this together. She easily sees the greatness in every other soul warrior because she knows if we have to go to spiritual battle with someone, we had better think highly of them.

TURNING IT AROUND

Even though spiritual wars are tough and necessary, they always bring some sort of gift. We may ask, "What kind of gift could incessant battling and suffering possibly bring me?" This is a legitimate question because it rarely feels like a gift when we are going through what feels like hell. But remember those three questions I asked earlier in the chapter? Well, we are going to turn them around and discover the goodness that spiritual wars can bring:

What gift am I willing to allow this circumstance or person to give me? As before, think in terms of spiritual and emotional assets, not physical ones.

What wonderful things am I now doing for others or allowing others to do for me in regard to this situation? Sometimes we put up walls that prevent others from giving us love and joy and vice versa. Spiritual wars are initiated by the spirit to tear down those barriers so that useless thought patterns can be done away with and more fruitful ones can take their place.

How am I living more as my authentic "self" right now? The answer to this question makes us look at how we are living out our value system and upholding our moral code while dealing with particular people and circumstances.

See how spiritual battles make us better people by helping us evolve into higher mind states? They exist to unleash ultimate wisdom. No matter what stage of evolution we are in, when we finally commit to becoming life-long soul warriors, we will move away from the mundane to eventual enlightenment.

SOUL AFFIRMATION

I have been called to active duty. My task is to be a defender of all things praiseworthy. First, I defend myself because I recognize my own virtue. Second, I defend others who may not yet know how good they really are. Though I may get warworn and need support sometimes, I know that the battle is mine and I must win it.

PART
—2—

RELATIONSHIPS

CHAPTER 5

SOUL RELATIONSHIPS

We are not held back by the love we didn't receive in the past,
but by the love we're not extending in the present.

—Marianne Williamson

Humans are hardwired to seek out meaningful connections. These connections come in many forms and have varying degrees of attachment based on whether someone is in the inner circle or outer circle.

People who populate our inner circles are the ones that we invest in. This investment is a serious commitment of energy, time, and intimacy. Inner circle people are the ones we call in the middle of the night when we need encouragement, who watch our kids if we have to work late and serve us homemade chicken soup when we have colds. Heck, they can even be counted on for a ride to the airport, and we know how big a deal that is.

Outer circle connections are more casual but still enhance our lives. Regardless of how much we see these people, we have some emotional *detachment*. They are more like acquaintances rather than close friends but can still be stimulating and fun. Sometimes outer circle connections are formed with members of organizations or groups we belong to. These are the people that help us reach collective goals.

But sometimes situations arise and cause us to re-evaluate the surface level purpose and value of our connections. We are forced to ask ourselves why other people *really* matter. The answer is because their very existence makes them the embodiment of miracles. Everyone's presence is so profound that, without even trying, we all affect each other physically, spiritually, and mentally. We all leave etheric and physical traces of ourselves that intermingle with others' minds, bodies, and souls. That's one of the reasons why it's so important to cultivate a spirit consisting of contentment, peace, and love within ourselves.

The entwining of our true selves and inner happiness is meant for outward expression as we join with others. In fact, contented and pleasant relationships have a higher purpose from the soul's perspective. The joy that radiates from these relationships is necessary in today's hectic world because there are so many of us living in disconnected states, leaving us depressed and unhappy.

For example, a woman lacking the genuine spirit of connection may seek false validation through social comparisons that arouse her competitive instincts. She rushes to social media, a world of constructed images which becomes a substitute for face-to-face interaction. No longer trained in how to interact with real life humans, she has no clue. She starts to take her cues from social media and treats others like she is a troll in some comments section. No one wants to associate with her, and she ends up alone.

However, when we have satisfying and peaceful bonds, the opposite happens. Soothing emotions and stability replace hostility and suspicion. Soulfully, we want to share, listen, and are comfortable enough to be vulnerable. Since people with high Emotion Quotient (EQ) care about others, their relationships and networks tend to have more meaning. That positivity radiates out and adds to all lives, giving even the most disconnected of us an opportunity to have a sense of belonging.

The buoyancy of meaningful connections is not only limited to the mind. They also improve our health. Hormones like the emotional bonding agent oxytocin and feel-good dopamine flood our bodies. Our hearts get stronger and immune systems receive a boost. But most importantly, relationships inspire us to take better care of ourselves because we have something good to live for.

But not all relationships are filled with sunshiny brightness. Relationships can expose our shadows. If you really want to know what is going on deep inside a person, take a look at their relationships. Relationships reveal what is suppressed in the heart and mind, such as unreleased traumas, self-esteem issues, and unforgiveness. To enter into any relationship, and be successful at it, requires a certain amount of a fearless consciousness.

Chances are that you are concerned with a particular type of relationship, whether it is with family members, a spouse, or friends. This particular chapter, however, is a general introduction to relationships. It only serves as a foundation for the specific relationships that we will talk about later on. So, let's get started.

ALONE-FULL

Since we're not bunny rabbits, we should stop jumping into relationships with others before we have created meaningful ones with ourselves. This jumping is a problem because these seemingly "organic" relationships wind up being triggers for our anger and fears. Certain people just seem to arouse those unexamined areas of our psyches, causing them to vibrate. Unlikeable parts of ourselves rise to the surface as we fight to push them back down.

As we battle against ourselves, it becomes increasingly difficult to give support, understanding, and love to the arouser of our emotional triggers. Simply put, our unmasked secret selves will not allow us to engage in a wholesome relationship. We become unstable, nasty, and unkind…or allow others to be that to us. Since we can't give what we don't have, there is no way to extend genuine peace, sisterhood, or any type of love to another.

Turmoil in relationships does have an upside, though. It reveals what we need to heal within ourselves. Once we uncover that, we will need to go deeper to understand and connect to the wounded inner child. Then we will be able to lay bare our souls and dissect those negative aspects that are lurking within us. Clearing out the muck gets us closer to the pristine condition we were born in.

There are innumerable blockages that any one person can have. These blocks ruin their ability to relate to others in a useful way. For instance, sometimes when women don't know how to relate to others, they give the impression that they just don't care and shut themselves off even more. But right now, let's focus on one blockage that seems to be a major contributor to destructive relationships: *not knowing the difference between being lonely and being alone.*

Lonely women have a void, they consider silence and stillness to be killers. Desperate to avoid being alone with themselves, they seek every measure to distract from boredom by medicating with noise: constant phone calls, TV, music, or crowds. But silence and stillness usually win out and force them to think about things that they avoid during noisy, frenetic moments.

However, silence can be golden. That same torturing silence is where that nagging, empty void resides. Going to the void to see what is missing can actually be the key to alleviating loneliness.

The flip side to loneliness is being alone. Typically, emotionally mature women enjoy their own company and are self-assured. They are *alone-full.* This type of fullness allows them to own themselves and maintain a deep connection to their souls. To them, joy and freedom spring from self-generated happiness. That is why alone-full does not equate isolation; it is rather immersing in the peace of selfhood.

Alone-full women do not shun others. They relish friends and family like anyone else. It's just that others are accents to their lives, not centerpieces. Alone-full women usually have their own thing, which gives them a chance to bask in their own light. These women's "things" are independently developed smarts, hobbies, and talents. They are always willing to add new "things" to their repertoire. Their ripened confidence makes them interesting not only to others, but they are interesting to themselves.

Furthermore, alone-full women don't emotionally drain others. They have learned how to work out their own problems, for the most part. However, even the most emotionally-stable women may need the help of their friends and loved ones from time to time. Women who relish alone time are not immune to stress, hardship, and even bouts of loneliness. There is no shame in that. Yet they don't allow themselves to get overrun with non-productive emotions for too long. Vowing not to be slaves to despair, they do the hard work of purging their regrets and sorrows. Then they are able to enjoy relationships filled with goodwill and giving from the heart because they aren't losing anything. In fact, the more they give, the more their supply is replenished.

MATURITY

Frankly, the formation of relationships can be hard, and sometimes we simply do not have the ability to rise to their challenges. We may cope by becoming mired in self-pity, blaming others, or denying our sad plights. However, some of us go to therapy and receive the proper treatment to aid in overcoming psychological demons. Others embrace a healthier lifestyle or expand their spiritual boundaries. But these situations are personal gains, something exclusive to the individual.

Sometimes, though, when we have grown personally, we think that is the end. We can mistakenly believe that we have achieved so much self-awareness that there is nothing else to learn. And what we could not or would not change about ourselves, we excuse by saying, "This is just who I am. Deal with it."

But relationships demand constant growth and change. There will always be areas of our psyches that need to be exposed and healed. If we have hubris, we will ignore the rest of the internal work we need to do and miss out on an exciting chance to mature.

Maturity is what we need to grow positively into who we *really* are and only serves in enhancing our personal relationships. Moreover, as we come to understand ourselves more fully, we are able to understand others.

It is all about progression versus regression. If we do not grow past comfy boundaries and allow those very boundaries to define us, we will not only become ineffective but move backwards. And if that happens, there is no way any more growth, love, or joy can occur.

COMPASSION

We have to give what we want to get. Everyone wants compassion given to them. Compassion is kindness and tenderness. Things like soft touching, using humor to brighten someone's day, dealing with people holistically (mind, body, soul), and being present (getting off the phone or computer when interacting) are ways to express compassion. Moreover, compassion prevents us from taking our friends and family for granted. It is honoring and taking care of others, especially when they are down.

When considering more intimate contacts, compassion does not exist to blindly tie us to others. We are compassionate by choice, and that choice comes with an understanding of reciprocity from both parties. If this reciprocity is not forthcoming, either party can leave at any time.

UNDERSTANDING

When we understand people, we can intuit their needs. We can sense when they need a little extra help or a superb listener. We are non-judgmental when they are relating parts of their lives to us. Acceptance of people enables us to understand their flaws and virtues because we recognize our own.

Understanding is especially important when it is difficult to extend warm feelings toward others. Some examples of these instances are when they are inconsiderate, depressed, or just being flat-out cantankerous. Pride tells us to snap back at them, that we do not have to take it. However, it is during those times when kindness, understanding, and respect really mean something.

SOCIAL INTELLIGENCE

Social intelligence is just simply being knowledgeable about human behavior. It automatically makes you study your own behavior which results in constant self-improvement. Flexibility plays a part in social intelligence, too. Flexibility is the ability to compromise. Compromising is not being a "yes" woman. It is, however, welcoming and adjusting to someone else's needs and being tolerant enough to go with their flow. Your tolerance will allow you to be empathic to someone else's present concerns and needs and to see the world through their eyes.

VULNERABILITY

Happy relationships require vulnerability. However, for some women vulnerability can be scary. They can see it as weakness, something to be preyed upon. But this does not have to necessarily be the case. Instead of viewing vulnerability as weakness, understand that it is really the courageous path in which our souls find deep connection to one another.

Vulnerability is not the same as gullibility. You can still maintain your intelligence and sovereignty as you open your heart to allow comradery or love to enter. In fact, vulnerability is a gateway to love because it helps you release your craving for fear-based connections.

As you experience your own personal freedom through vulnerability, you become more in tune with other people's desire for the same freedom. This freedom can be defined as a sense of connection that allows us to be who we really are without retribution. This freedom flows in a circuit, going from sender to receiver and vice versa. Moreover, the freedom of vulnerability helps us to release the fear of being seen as imperfect. It is about self-acceptance as well as the acceptance of others. We feel relaxed enough to be human and still be loved.

Although vulnerability requires bravery and trust, a certain amount of detachment must be exercised. After all, there are people who will try to take advantage of you, and that is why it is so important to scrutinize people before you let them fully enter your life. Until they have proven themselves to be worthy, act with caution. This is not paranoia or mistrusting the process; it is just part of the reality of being a discerning woman.

"SO, WHAT ARE YOUR CREDENTIALS?"

You may have to interact with family, but everyone else must qualify. Someone expecting to have any type of relationship with you must bring something of value to the table called relationship credentials. Why? Because you've worked hard at becoming the best "you" and should not be expected to lower your expectations for someone who has not done the same.

High and proper standards are logic based, but nuanced judgment must be used. Some women cut off many people by mistakenly believing they are setting standards. But what they are really doing is acting out of vindictiveness or supposed superiority. The act of ostracizing is a way of stooping to a very low level, trying to make someone feel unworthy of even a response. Therefore, the motivations behind your boundary setting will reveal your emotional management ability and character.

However, as a soulful woman, you will set standards with a soft heart and graceful soul. You'll still enter into relationships with high expectations for receiving loving-kindness yet have a willingness to give the same thing yourself. You'll have pure motives and only seek relationships that affirm goodness.

SETTING BOUNDARIES

You start by setting boundaries, not only for others but also yourself. Your boundaries are a form of emotional management that will protect your soul from encroachment from others who would do you harm. Boundaries preserve you from trauma or living with a constant sense of dread. Boundaries protect by helping you recognize the first signs of trouble like offhand remarks or sly insults.

Boundaries will also prevent you from letting others test you to see how far they can go. You won't let them because you will stop (1) minimalizing their bad behavior and (2) no longer accept their bogus apologies. Without enforcement, others will only continue to ignore your fragile boundaries and their behavior will grow more insidious. Eventually, you will have no choice but to either break off the relationship or become desensitized to it.

Though I just gave you some examples, you will have to develop your own standards. But no matter what criteria you list, remaining faithful to it can be difficult. You may be tempted to give some leeway or make exceptions.

To avoid trouble, you have to manage your emotions. Emotional management is an excellent tool to use when qualifying people for relationships. If we want to know how well we've been qualifying in the past, we can start by looking at who we spend our time with. This will determine not only who they are, but who we are.

Motivational speaker Jim Rohn stated, *You are the average of the five people you spend the most time with.* In other words, who you spend your time with has an effect on your life. And over time, we develop patterns (unconscious habits) concerning the persons we choose to associate with.

Excluding family, think about those five people you hang out with the most. How did you consciously or unconsciously qualify them? Did you enter into relationships with them based on emotionally driven reasons? How is that working for you?

Your relationships have probably taught you that others' behaviors and feelings are highly contagious viruses which give good or bad results. Taking that knowledge into the future will make you more aware of what other people are doing, acknowledging that their behavior may have an effect on yours.

KINDNESS

After you've cultivated the characteristics that will enable you to make connections and qualify people, you must master a particular action—kindness. Kindness is a word often spoken about yet is one of the least performed. It is so much easier to think about acting kind instead of existing as a kind *BEING*. Before we go any further, let's take a moment to get a clear understanding of what kindness is.

Kindness is the outward expression of tolerance and goodwill through speech and action. However, even though we are kind beings, who we should give kindness to is tricky. This is because we don't interact exclusively with people we know, intimately or casually. We must venture out into the world where we encounter all sorts of strangers. These interactions are short-lived, not allowing time to vet. So, it is best to err on the side of general kindness most of the time. When you make it a priority to engage in general kindness, your overall quality of life will be enhanced. Niceties are almost always immediately returned. However, the best part is that those random pleasantries and courtesies seem to have a rippling effect. By the end of the day, many people can be touched by your one random act of kindness, and you won't regret making someone else's life a little happier and easier.

TYPES OF KINDNESS

Listed below are a few types of kindnesses. They reveal how to interact with those around us and are displayed emotionally or physically. As you read through the list, keep in mind that the physical acts are sometimes easier than the emotional ones because feelings call upon more spiritual resources. Once the physical act is performed, it is over. However, heartfelt emotions are extremely powerful and have profound impacts by creating holy bonds.

FORGIVENESS

We've talked a lot about forgiveness. But it really is the foundation of so many good things. All of our relationships consist of three entities (us, the other person, and God). Forgiveness releases not only our pain but also the pain of the other person and even God's pain for us. After forgiveness has been given, we can allow God to freely move within our hearts and lighten our minds.

VOCALIZING SOMEONE'S GOODNESS

Everyone likes hearing their name in conjunction with something good. This is especially true if they are caught in a moment of self-doubt. During those down times, a melancholy person needs someone who can help them rise above their negative thoughts, and a kind woman is the right one for the job. A kind woman can step in and testify about someone's merits and worthiness. She eagerly reminds the self-doubter of her strengths and virtues, building her mental legs until she can stand on her own. However, this is not simple hype; it is based on the actuality of that person's goodness. It is only speaking the truth back into reality.

EQUALIZING WITH OPEN-NESS

If you feel comfortable, you can reveal your own struggles to demonstrate that you aren't perfect. You can reveal as much or as little as you want, but the point is to be relatable and transparent. When you are open, the need to put on airs is removed and affinity occurs. You and the other person are free to be perfectly imperfect and that leads to more individual self-acceptance. It's so nice to come to the conclusion that there is truly no superior or inferior. We are all the same.

REALNESS

Being authentic is also a way to perform the act of kindness. Pretending to be someone else or espousing values that you don't believe in perpetrates a fraud, and a fraud is a lie. It is unkind to lie to another person because it validates you can't be trusted. However, an authentic woman can be trusted. Her points of view may not be accepted by all, but she knows how to express them in reasonable, non-offensive ways. In other words, she does not believe free speech is a legitimate reason to bully, condescend, arouse fear, or make fun of others. Her intelligent-based authenticity inspires comfort and a sense of safety, even with people who have opposing opinions.

LOVE

This is kindness at its height. Love is not only an emotion; it is an action. It is a choice to be patient, understanding, affectionate, and tolerant. Love gives out copious amounts of appreciation and joy, too. At the same time, love necessitates self-control as it is not dependent on animal instinct and base emotions. It requires a lofty outlook held by a woman determined to find good and give good to the world.

RELUCTANT KINDNESS

Kindness sounds good, but sometimes we just don't want to give it. These times usually occur when we feel we've been hurt or slighted by someone. The last thing we want to do is give that person some kindness in exchange for the rude, crude, and sometimes sadistic behavior that they gave us.

Kindness is a skill and is usually mastered when it's easier *not* to be nice to someone. To be kind is also a choice we make when someone has hurt us. The choice is to either give into the ego's desire to metaphorically (or literally) slap someone in the face or soften our anger. Obviously, it is better to take the focus off the temporary gratification retaliation would bring. We must be mindful that our anger may cost us our future happiness and success.

Even when we reluctantly extend kindness to someone who has hurt us, it allows for our soul to cultivate more personal happiness. This happiness comes not from the other person; it comes from the act of giving and God. That is what makes this happiness so wonderful; it is part of our earthly destiny. Therefore, it makes us live in the trans-formative way we were meant to. Knowledge helps us move closer to becoming whole through dealing with the trials others put us through.

Once we move past reluctant kindness and embrace genuine kindness, we put God on display. He shows up in every interaction we have. Our willingness to be kind shows who we are really trying to please—our souls and God.

TALK TIME

If a man's heart is rankling with discord and ill feeling toward you, you can't win him to your way of thinking with all the logic in Christendom. Scolding parents and domineering bosses and husbands and nagging wives ought to realize that people don't want to change their minds. They can't be forced or driven to agree with you or me. But they may possibly be led to, if we are gentle and friendly, ever so gentle and ever so friendly.—Dale Carnegie

This is a fantastic quote. Communication is right up there with forgiveness in terms of relationship functionality. And like forgiveness, it is something we fail at a lot.

Communication falls into two distinct patterns—destructive and constructive. *Destructive communication* is when we attack our companions, making them feel unworthy. This is a hobbling technique that comes under many guises…nagging, belittling, and screaming as you finger-point and invade someone's personal space.

Yes, we want to be strong, empowered women; but sometimes we confuse coming off as bitter and hateful with getting our point across with conviction. Just like we don't want others lecturing and wearing us down with their destructive communication, we have to think about how we would feel if we were the recipient of our own negative attitude. On the other hand, we should make a point to avoid reactive people whose only method of communicating is through explosive flare-ups, shutting us out, and/or name calling. Whether the negativity is perpetrated by us or someone else, destructive communication is guaranteed to tear at the fabric of a relationship until both people feel alienated and whatever goodwill there was is gone.

Constructive communication is a builder of stable relationships. If you are confused about what constructive communication is, just think about how you would like to be addressed or spoken to. Even if there is an argument or difference of opinion, you would want another person to remain calm and be patient with you. You would still want to feel respected and honored after the exchange. Constructive communication is about coming from a place of grace and sincerity. It is speaking up about what our needs are while neither person lives in fear over the other's reaction.

Before you approach a sensitive subject, remember these four steps:

(1) disarm by taking a step back and bringing the intensity level down,

(2) always use a loving approach,

(3) remember to honor the person in front of you, and

(4) make sure you listen attentively and carefully.

As you apply these four actions, make sure you speak slowly and softly and do not monopolize the conversation. Express whatever you are feeling and allow the other person the space to make things right. All feelings in a healthy interaction should be validated; this is an obvious component of a healthy relationship.

The thing is, we all know what to do to foster productive communication. The problem is that we would rather *not* do it. Sometimes effective communication is difficult to master because it requires a relinquishing of the ego. It is simply easier to blow off steam or pout. But more than that, we have a tendency to get caught up in win-lose debates. Our egos tell us to crush our opponent so that we will somehow feel superior; we are so afraid of vulnerability.

Egos block effective communication by making us think we are superior to everyone else. After all, the ego's world is nothing but competition. But those same egos have caused many women's inflated pride to have dinner alone with only their obnoxious mouths to keep them company.

Why are we so invested in the win instead of the process of effective communication? It is because we have the uncanny ability to only see the "me" in the situation and focus on the survival of our self-aggrandizement. The Golden Rule ("Do unto others as you would have them do unto you.") flies out the window because it only works when we truly treat others like we want to be treated. However, the more invested we are in winning, the more we lose concern for the other person. The ego does not care how we treat them but expects to be treated well and wants to win at all cost because it feels that being right is the prize. Revenge, an I-told-you-so attitude, or having the last word are the ego's markers, and it doesn't mind believing in a false reality that says it won.

But the thing about the ego is that it is consumed with fear and terribly afraid of being exposed as weak. And if a sane person exposes it as the troublemaker it is, that same person will not hesitate to eradicate it. To prevent this, the ego strives to perpetuate conflict to prove that its existence is valid.

We have to corral the ego to co-exist with one another. Effective communication is methodical, not manipulative. It is orderly as opposed to rambunctious. It helps people see each other's side of an issue and is beneficial to both. But to achieve positive communication, you have to be willing to choose peace. This is done by letting others express themselves without taking their opinion personally.

An ego-less woman strives to be understood instead of proving her point. She appreciates everyone's point of view, knowing that their way of looking at the world does not devalue hers. She moves on from disagreements with grace and more knowledge than she had before. Her communication is an exchange of love rather than an excuse to talk.

IT WAS WORTH IT, THOUGH

Before we move into specific types of relationships, let's take this time to accept that all of them can be challenging. But when seen from a higher perspective, relationships are a beautiful way to gain emotional maturity and knowledge of self. Relationships show us where we need to grow or how we have evolved into a standard bearer that others can emulate. Every interaction is an opportunity to express our authenticity, kindness, and mercy. Sure, we risk hurt and rejection. But all experience is valuable and can be put to good use. Ultimately, it is better to have had the chance to experience other souls than not have had it at all.

SOUL AFFIRMATION

My love is not meant to be hoarded inside of me. It is an extension of the affection I have for myself, shared with everyone I come in contact with. Yes, there will be times when my ego tells me to keep my love or only give it to those who serve me. But my soul will nudge me toward the truth. And the truth is that I can never lose love because the more I give, the more it grows in my heart.

CHAPTER 6

SOUL MATE

*Your divine mate already exists. When you get to the place in
yourself that is peaceful divine love your true mate will be revealed.*

—Iyanla Vanzant

What do you first think of when you hear the term soul mate? Most
of us have been conditioned from childhood to think of a soul mate in
purely romantic terms. We envision a Prince Charming who becomes
our magical other half, embodying the wondrous traits that we have
disowned or are unaware of. We imagine that these ideal partners will
make us feel good and happy to be alive. That is why we "love" the
popular concept of what a soul mate is, for its romantic notions.

However, romantic love is often true love's window dressing and sometimes can actually be opposite from it. It's often based on lust, neediness, and unrealistic expectations. We realize this when the dream-like state of infatuation wears off and idealized forms disappear, and we are faced with a real person. Nonetheless, this is an opportunity for true love to occur.

We must first understand that the differences between romantic and true love are pronounced. Romantic love is often preferable to true love. Romantic love gives exhilarating pumps of adrenaline and pleasurable tingles in the belly. It's about being high on hormones and feeling like you can walk on water. Flowers, candy, mind-blowing sex…really, who doesn't want that?

But true love depends on a soul mate kind of bond. This type of love is about *doing* instead of *feeling*. Rose-colored glasses are removed, and the prescription bifocals are put on so that the transcendent nature of love can be discovered. True love is seeing beauty in someone despite their ugliness. True love is seeing the bravery in someone despite their fear. True love is seeing goodness in someone despite their hate.

True love, as great as it is, can be hard. It is an act of great faith. You'll need this faith to summon the tremendous strength and courage necessary to experience the fullness of another human being. Faith will shield you when integrity, sincerity, and fortitude are tested. Moreover, faith will help you understand that true love is the ultimate service because *sometimes* extreme circumstances demand you give with every cell of your body without getting anything in return. That is why receiving true love is such a blessing.

MALE AND FEMALE

You know who your ideal man is. He's physical perfection and has the most awesome personality. He's the sole object populating your lazy-day fantasies. You saw bits of him materialized through other men. Alas, they failed to measure up completely to your flawless prototype, and the relationships ended.

But if you take some time to reflect and list all the traits your perfect man has, you'll realize that those are the traits of your inner "male" self. Your inner male is akin to an animus. Your picture of your ideal man is actually your unrecognized sexual shadow. And we all want to fully merge with the shadow.

In a sense, we've already merged with our shadows. All humans are a mixture of male and female energies, and we need both to properly navigate the world. However, the body, psychological propensities, and culture define your outer visage as man or woman, and how that visage is defined is mostly how we live. Now, we're not talking about sexual preferences or if behavior can be artificially induced. We are, however, making an observation about polarity, specifically male and female. However, purely feminine or masculine people rarely exist.

Generally, biological women veer toward degrees of femininity and men toward degrees of masculinity. Some women have learned how to blend these energies in certain areas of their lives. Successful businesswomen, for instance, are a beautiful combination of both, displaying yin and yang.

However, the balancing of energies is tricky when it comes to modern-day relationships. In present times, self-reflection is necessary. How is your masculine energy typically used? Most likely, it pushes you forward, understands and operates through the intellect using quantitative data, and sometimes uses force to get its way.

Now, let's apply that to relationships. For instance, if you've been using your masculine energy properly in relationships, it has probably helped you become a better communicator. Whenever you need to communicate a troubling issue with your beloved, it is best to approach using positive male energy. This is done through the use of a controlled, rational manner that is devoid of emotionality (nagging, dramatics, or hostility). If your partner understands the logic behind your words and how changing or performing a task for you can benefit them, they will be much more apt to listen and do what you want them to do. Moreover, you can better listen to their point of view with a more open mind and not take it as a personal attack. You may even discover that they have some legitimate criticism.

But that same masculine energy can be misused. When this happens, you can become aggressive, rude, or even violent toward your partner. For example, you may be tempted to prepare a rebuttal before he or she is even finished giving their side. However, if in that instance, you do not like what was said, it is better to think before responding. You may have to come close to biting off your tongue to avoid an instinctive retort. But words spoken can't be taken back and can cause irreparable damage. Proper use of masculinity is learning to tolerate discomfort, especially in uncomfortable conversations. Just absorb what is said, think about it, and then make a high road response. That is the difference between responding and dismissing.

You now have a better idea of how your masculine energy can help you maintain a calm, detached attitude when dealing with stressful communication in your relationship. However, if someone's language is abusive, your inner "He" (and your inner bitch) will give you the courage to stand up for yourself and leave.

Let's now delve into the womanly side of our nature. Feminine energy has the remarkable power to change events and people with the use of softness. It does this by helping you read people and understand what they may need, even when they don't know themselves.

Femininity requires a high EQ—a distinctive feminine trait—to understand and integrate higher emotions. This is because it utilizes wisdom as opposed to intellect and knows how to give instead of to take. Your EQ also gives you the ability to balance your polar (male/female) mindset as it relates to love. In other words, the feminine allows you to cultivate a complimentary relationship between both poles. Then you can properly internalize your male as you externalize your female when dealing with the opposite gender. Using your logical male mind, clear reasoning will be your guide as you express your girly self.

However, feminine energy can be misused, too. It can make you complacent, a doormat, and send you down the path of self-annihilation. Moreover, female energy is too often mistaken for weakness, when its effects are actually more penetrating and long-lasting than the excessive use of male energy. If you try to suppress feminine energy, you are in danger of becoming a woman who thrives on strife and hardship.

Being a complete human being requires balance. Successful integration of your female and male energies gives you the ability to attract positive events and people, and you'll more easily remove opposition to your desires. You will also be less inclined to search *with-out* for what you should be looking for *with-in*. Then you'll truly be not only the queen but also the king of your *inner* realm.

YOUR FIRST SOUL MATE

What is the mastery of your female and male energies *really* about? See, no matter how good you look, the effort you have put into cultivating an effervescent personality, college degrees you have earned or the money you make, you will not be liked or desired by everyone. But you are not concerned with everyone: you are only concerned with The One.

Who is this One?

The One is you.

You are your very first soul mate—the beautiful queen inwardly possessed by an all-knowing king, totally *loving* and *in love* with yourself. Your pure self-love is not arrogant or narcissistic; it is actually exalted.

When you have a romance with yourself, you teach yourself how you want to be treated and loved. Therefore, spoil the lover inside of you. Pamper yourself; go on dream vacations and out to fine dinners. Appreciate all the curves of your body. Be in awe of your talents and how you've overcome challenges. Practice constant self-care on all levels of your being.

You will then fix in your mind what kind of behavior you expect from potential suitors and not allow anyone to treat you less than you'd treat yourself. I know, that sounds cliché. But before you cue the violins, let me remind you that what seems trite is actually time-honored wisdom. You, as a soul mate, must be equipped to handle the rigors of being in a relationship. But before you get there, you've got to love yourself.

A lack of self-love makes you enter a relationship empty and broken while hoping that the man you love will fill and fix you. You become nothing more than a vortex, siphoning life from your partner. Dependency makes you clingy and anxious. You never feel emotionally safe and act with suspicion. Abandonment issues arise, contributing to the deterioration of the relationship. Dependency never brings happiness because at its core is a fear of loss. When you think you are going to lose someone, you are willing to become the scapegoat or fatted calf. Therefore, you take responsibility for their faults and mistakes just to keep them around.

Interdependence is different, though. Interdependence is an exchange between two whole, sane individuals. Whole women seek interdependence and enter relationships with that *alone-full* state of mind we talked about earlier. Using their own mind power, they know how to calm and soothe themselves, and they can be there for someone else at the same time.

Because soulful women know how to satisfy their own needs, they have no desire to enter relationships prematurely, especially with men who are more interested in the chase than a relationship. After all, no woman should have to sacrifice her soul—lose her worth—to gain the fickle attention of another. Fortunately, a soulful woman is like garlic to vampires. Though not foolproof, vampiric people will smell her alone-fullness and most likely be warded off. Only the most brazen bloodsucker will test her. Alone-fullness makes you remember that your most glorious love supply comes from God, your soul, and yourself.

THE KNOWLEDGABLE ONE

It is one thing to have knowledge; it is another thing to apply it. When it comes to relationships, we sometimes have a tendency to believe they can be managed by simply following the steps in a book or the advice of well-meaning loved ones…all theoretical knowledge. But all too often, when we actually have to apply the theories, failure is the result.

This is due to the fact that we are often driven by emotion rather than logic and are rarely detached. Also, the simple application of concepts fails to take into account the nebulous nuances of relating to another human being. We end up being fueled by the ego and stoked by triggers. We ruminate on our partners' faults, and pride makes us dig in our heels and stonewall.

However, these tempting behaviors only give short-term grat-ification. They are choices born out of a lack of awareness and are devastating to our personal relationships. They set up events that cause resentment or hate. In these situations, the very air around us thickens, and we suffocate with depression.

For knowledge to go from theoretical to practical, it must be applied—not haphazardly—but with understanding and wisdom. To understand is to know the reasons why certain behaviors are useful. Wisdom is the growth incurred by applying those useful behaviors. Understanding and wisdom help us advance past childish feelings and automatic reactions. We mature.

Maturity is spectacular in its ability to open our minds and change our thinking patterns. Because our thoughts dictate our actions, mature thoughts make us more willing to treat our mates with compassion, even if we sometimes have to be firm. Essentially, good thoughts and feelings lead us to perform loving actions—actions of the soul.

Soul mates aren't found; they're made. Their love and commit-ment to each other are developed and refined over time. If you do reach this level, understand you are performing holy work. You will be a priestess of love.

WE ARE WHO WE ARE

There will be days when even the best soul mate is not lovable. Annoying habits, stinking attitudes, and personality flaws can drive us up the wall. Many times we are left thinking, *OMG! What have I done being with this person?*

As much as we evolve, there is still a core self. And we must remember that we can't change someone else's core self. Some peculiarities are immovable; that's why we're unique. Inborn personality traits can be downright annoying, though. For example, some people seem to have been born to argue, and they will be that way from cradle to grave. Moreover, there will always be controversial ideas that all of us doggedly hold on to, especially if we were indoctrinated during childhood. These become part of our identity. Some core identifiers can be religion, ethnic pride, aversions, and attractions. And ideas set in childhood can be terribly difficult to undo as they are wired into the brain.

It just so happens that when we first become involved with people, we get diluted versions of who they really are. We find their watered-down traits to be exciting or interesting…at the beginning. But, after a few months or years, people become more comfortable and gradually show us the uncensored version of who they are. Those slightly annoying habits become total nuisances. Cute peculiarities morph into major irritants.

Generally, the switch is not sudden. We can see the changeover taking place, but we usually ignore it or make excuses. Therefore, we have to accept responsibility for being in agreement. With that in mind, it's unfair to expect someone to change into something they are not. Sure, they may try to accommodate our requests for a while, but they will break like a pretzel from trying to bend. Eventually, if they really don't see the need to change, they will rebel.

Relationship check-ins are vitally important for warding off trouble before it starts. Emotionally mature couples try their best to avoid letting little problems become monumental ones. Toxic feelings and actions can be managed, and the relationship can go forward, having grown a little more.

However, in the end, we are still who we are. No matter how much we may grow as a couple, we still have parts inside of us that will never change. Some of those parts are spectacularly awesome, and some are ridiculously awful. It is what it is. No one is perfect and nor should they be expected to be.

Just as we would want others to see the beauty in us, we need to do that for our beloved. There will always be something in them that we respect and admire, and it is important to keep this in mind, especially when it gets tough. It can be a battle sometimes to like someone when they are disagreeable. But this is when we have to go from emotionally loving them when it's easy to consciously loving them when it's hard.

Conscious loving is a choice. Conscious loving is an action. Conscious loving serves them, not us. When we consciously love our partner, we are giving them security and showing that we can be trusted.

Does this mean downplaying our own needs? Accepting the behavior of an abuser? Not having a right for self-preservation? Of course, not.

All of us are expected to love ourselves, too. However, it is best not to get all bothered over the small stuff. We have to accept that certain parts of our loved ones are not going to change. If we fight against that, we will certainly be met with resistance.

Take a moment to think about how you feel when someone takes you as you are.

It feels good when someone sees you in the way God made you. Just admit that you're magnetized to people who acknowledge your wondrous self, even when you blunder. And the higher purpose of relationships is to give that same experience back to someone else.

SOUL MATE DEDICATION

There is a big difference between being involved with someone and being soul mate *committed*. When you are just merely involved, there are plenty of options. Since you have not made any requirements or agreements, you have the freedom to leave at any time without any moral obligation. You are just having a good time.

On the other hand, when you are soul mate committed, you are making a choice not to take advantage of your partner, abandon them in their time of need, and typically agree to be monogomous. Also, you have the mentality of *wanting* to work through your issues and *doing* the work to achieve that. Honoring someone is easier to do when a conscious decision for loyalty has been made. But to be loyal, you must have a moral code. Your moral code will incite your guilt if you are ever tempted to violate it, hopefully preventing you from messing up.

Sadly, the part about the work is where most people fail. Take disagreements, for example. Though we *want* to have effective communication, many of us want to be right even more. The *work* part of this equation comes by admitting your fault in the argument and apologizing for that. When you are no longer invested in being right, forgiveness and peace are allowed to stream in. You will likely find your partner also admitting their fault in the argument and receive an apology as well. It comes down to whether or not you want to co-exist tranquilly. In matters of the heart, being right does not always mean being peaceful; you've got to know which battles to fight.

Some women see glaring problems in the beginning of their relationship but decide to go forward anyway. This stems from the fear of being alone and feeling unloved. It then becomes their hope that the issues will somehow clear up or that their lover will change. The truth is this: what was bad before the commitment will be even worse after it.

Committing to another person should never be taken lightly. By the time you are ready to take this step, you should make sure that your foundation is strong and secure. It will form the basis for a healthy relationship with your significant other. It will hold steady when things get tough; after all, no relationship is always easy.

Listening is a great way we dedicate ourselves to our soul mates. It's hearing what someone is saying without internalizing it as a criticism. Sometimes what is heard as a slight is really someone expressing their core values, and discernment will prevent snapbacks at perceived negative criticisms. However, if we are unclear about someone's intentions, we should ask them what they meant. If they are expressing their values, we make sure they know we heard them and respect their value system while maintaining ours. Also, "When I hear you say…," or "What I'm hearing is…" are great non-combative phrases to convey that we are listening.

Additionally, as a soul mate, you must also be cognizant of the way someone likes to receive love. Some conflicts stem from lovers expressing love in a way different than the other prefers. Some of the ways people like to be shown love are praise, date nights, hugs, or little "happies" or gifts and acts of appreciation. As a dedicated soul mate, it is your job to figure out how your lover likes to be loved. But most people are thankful when their loved one does "regular work." Things like taking out the trash, cooking dinner, and going to work are important. Other tasks include being financially supportive, offering emotional comfort and sage advice, encouraging life dreams, or helping out with the logistics of everyday life. These services aren't mandates; they are performed willingly. Remember, soul mates perform services with a giving heart, not begrudgingly because of unwanted obligation.

Finally, there is evolution. Though some things stay the same, partners should grow and change together. They can take on new interests that they can share. Also, individually, as one partner positively expands, the other one should make sure to do the same. The combination of couple and individual evolution prevents one partner from outgrowing the other. Plus, it adds excitement by allowing each soul mate to get a *new* lover every once in a while.

Just keep in mind that people are not overly-complex creatures. Their needs in a relationship are very simple. They want to be admired. They want to be cared for. They want to be respected. They want to feel valued. And a woman who is willing to commit at the soul mate level is happy to do those things for her loved one.

THE GAMES WE PLAY

Going to the playground was one of the best parts of being a kid. The playground was a miniature fantasy world, filled with all sorts of neat toys and where adventure awaited. We were only limited by our imaginations as we ran wild and indulged in games such as hide and seek, hopscotch, and tag. Really, how many of us haven't been clotheslined during a game of Red Rover?

Though our kiddie games were fun, they also served a purpose. They taught us lessons about fair play, cooperation, how to win gracefully, and take a loss with dignity. Those same lessons can be used in our adult lives when we dedicate ourselves to another person. But the rules of engagement depend on what type of game we choose to play, and as adults, we typically choose tug-of-war.

The innocence of childhood made tug-of-war fun. There usually were no hard feelings, even if someone yanked you into the dirt. Just like the childhood game, tug-of-war for adults pits two people against each other. However, instead of pulling a rope and maintaining goodwill, they contentiously pull on opposite ends of an idea. The objective is to use strength—whether that strength is verbal, intellectual, or emotional—to overwhelm the other person.

There are times when tug-of-war is required and/or inevitable, but those instances are rare. More often than not, it's more prudent to avoid playing tug-of-war at all. Once the hard line is drawn, it's difficult for soul mates to reach a compromise as both parties are too entrenched in their ideology. Soul mates then grab the metaphorical rope and begin furiously yanking back and forth as each of them sinks into victim mode. When soul mates get to this point, they feel less connected to each other. If this happens too often, they can feel like the relationship "itself" is wrong and may long for a way out. Moreover, if the delusion of soul mate perfection has permeated the relationship, deep frustration occurs. They both drop the rope and go off in opposite directions.

The thing is, we tend to have an idealistic view of what soul mate relationships are. The romanticized notion of soul mates is presented as a synchronization of our intentions, desires, and tendencies—that we should be a perfect match all the time without any sort of push or pull.

But life happens, and if two individuals live together long enough, they reach plenty of impasses. Rarely is a relationship functioning at an optimum 100/100 percent level. Relationships are fluid, in constant flux with participants switching off being the giver or taker. Some people accept this and go with the flow. However, in some circumstances, giving or receiving can be detrimental. For example, if one person is always the giver, resentment can occur. Conversely, if someone feels like they are on the bottom or being rescued all the time, competition may set in.

The operative word in tug-of-war is *war*. It's all about battle. Not many soul mates can sustain the dynamics of such a relationship and will crack under the pressure. How about we stop playing destructive games? Let's head on over to the swing set and just play instead.

When we sit next to each other on two swings, we start at ground level…just like in real life, we, as a couple, have a starting point. We look at each other, laughing and talking, and then we start to swing back and forth. This is equivalent to living a life together and achieving positive relationship milestones, and pretty soon, like swinging, we soar.

Other times, only one of us is on the swing. The other one is the helper who gives gentle pushes, helping the swinger rise, like when we are supporting each other.

Then sometimes, when we want to be extra close, we swing on one swing, together (double swinging). We face each other with one swinger's legs straddling the other's hips. This way we experience true intimacy, not sexuality. The goal is not to soar high (no outward goal to achieve), because when we double swing, getting high up is physically hard to do. What we are really doing is re-establishing our commitment to be together.

But it must be said that swinging requires vulnerability. Just like playground swinging, specifically double swinging, both partners rely on each other's movements. They must feel safe enough to work together to create a comfortable rhythm. Also, when one is on the swing and the other is the pusher, the pusher must be considerate enough not to push the swinger too hard, as this could make them fall off. And the pusher definitely should not push the swinger too high because this would cause fear. True soul mates would never dream of creating this kind of emotional trauma for another person.

No matter how you decide to play, being with your beloved can bring out the kid in you—either the insolent child or the merry cherub. Hopefully, you'll get on that swing set and experience that awesome moment when both of you get the feeling of flying free. That is truly the magical moment that you'll know the wonder of being in love with your best friend.

NOT YOUR TYPICAL BANK

Every love relationship possesses what would be the equivalent of a bank account. Think of it as a love account. The difference between the two is that instead of dealing with greenbacks and coins, the love account contains love, energy, and acts of service.

Just like a regular bank account, you have to be diligent when it comes to the love account's deposits and withdrawals. Soul mates strive for functioning relationships based on the voluntary give and take of the two people involved (deposits and withdrawals, respectively). Small daily deposits into each other's accounts are essential. These frequent goodies give us something to look forward to and contribute to the overall success of the relationship.

However, special or emergency situations may call for rather large deposits to be put into the other person's account. The more each partner is committed to making the other one happy, the greater the balances in both their accounts grow. The key is for both partners to make more deposits than withdrawals. When this happens, accounts flourish.

It is normal to enjoy the deposits. It feels good when our beloved is attentive, affectionate, and takes care of our needs. That is part of being in a sound relationship. Enjoying this kind of behavior is not selfish. Being able to accept loving-kindness from your beloved demonstrates a healthy sense of self-worth. It also means that you are appreciative of the blessings that another person is bestowing upon you.

Usually, it does not take much effort to deposit into someone else's love account. A simple text to see how their day is going, picking up the dry cleaning, or giving a heartfelt hug are some small ways to fill the coffers. Though gifts are wonderful, it is a rare human that constantly needs extreme material reward to feel appreciated. For most, a little courtesy and warmth go a long way.

There are also more substantial ways to deposit into someone's love account. For example, you can honor your beloved's values. You don't have to value the same things but honoring your lover's value system should be a priority. Another way to make a deposit is to communicate with fairness and understanding; this will aid in avoiding emotional triggers. Also, when you take responsibility for your actions, you make deposits. This also helps you better yourself.

Nonetheless, there will be days when making that deposit may seem difficult, like right after an argument. It may be hard to give courtesy and respect at times, but it must be done. You will have to summon humility to assist you, but you can do it.

Also, transfers from someone else's account into yours are sometimes necessary. You aren't expected to always be strong, and life can sometimes get you down. These are the moments when you may need more love or support from your beloved. But if you receive these love funds too frequently or for minor things, you are in danger of stepping into the realm of selfishness and dependency. Think about it: What would happen if you constantly withdrew from someone's account and never made a deposit? Or how would you feel if they never made a deposit but took advantage of your goodness? That would result in a zero or negative balance.

There are many ways to take love account balances into the red. Being overly critical and mean when communicating are ways to throw away love funds. These two factors can cause your partner to become defensive or turn away. Other destroyers of love funds are gaslighting, vengeance, pent-up resentment, and passive-aggressive behavior. Finally, being dismissive of your lover's concerns or opinions will cause your currency to disappear.

Negative behaviors cause love checks to bounce all over the place. Hurt feelings, anger, and resentment are the fees that have to be paid. Those fees are expensive as they cause untold damage to your relationship. There may not be enough love currency in the world that can replenish your account after that.

Viewing soul mate love as an account allows you to monitor how you interact and respond to your beloved. It gives you a meaningful understanding about how the way you choose to give and receive either helps or hinders your relationship. The deposits may grow slowly, but as long as they rise on the graph, your relationship stands at least a chance at success.

Occasionally, you may encounter some "meltdowns" and scary dwindling of the account's balance. But just as a nation overcomes the trials and tribulations of a rough economy, soul mates triumph over difficulties in relationships. You and your partner may have to ride it out. Just remember, that it takes two mindful, responsible, and *willing* people to do so. After "I'm sorry" has been said, it is time to put the words into action. "I'm sorry" doesn't matter unless coupled with a change in behavior. Let your apology be experienced through your actions rather than relying on moving lips.

EMOTIONAL BANKRUPTCY

We diligently tend to our monetary bank accounts, knowing where every nickel and dime goes. Peace of mind comes when we are in the black. Soul mates treat their love bank accounts the same way. They make sure they are receiving and giving an abundance of love but are careful with whom they perform the exchange with.

However, some of us choose to recklessly gamble with the funds in our accounts. We choose high-risk men who are almost guaranteed to leave destruction in their wake. But most destructive men don't appear to be that way at the beginning. However, there is a man that we know right from the start is bad for us. Who am I talking about?

Taken men. These are men with current girlfriends or wives. As far as your love bank goes, this man will not only leave you overdrawn but with bad credit and bankruptcy. Deep inside, you know the object of your lust used a form of a confidence trick to draw you in. In the end, the love you gave him is a sunk cost. So why is it, even though we know the danger, some of us still act like we have love money to burn?

Only the most manipulative and maniacal women ever truly intend to entice a man with a committed girlfriend or wife. In fact, most affairs start innocently enough. Two people are brought together by some circumstance. One is a single woman and the other one is a taken man. Once in each other's presence, there may be an erotic spark. Some flirtation highlighted by compliments and maybe even some "accidental" touching occurs. The conversations are light and breezy, and each of you finds the other to be absolutely intriguing.

Soon, more boundaries are crossed—consciously or subconsciously. Secret emails turn into sneaky lunches. Clandestine lunches turn into movie nights. Hush-hush movie nights turn into evenings at a hotel or the single woman's home. The next thing you know, the woman is embroiled in a tempestuous affair. She gives him all the money in her love account, taking out high interest loans for what she can't cover.

If you allow yourself to be enticed like that, you might as well be under a spell. The hocus pocus of your lover's magic wand (wink) has totally bewitched you. If you are involved with a married man, that ring on that left ring finger can be especially hypnotizing. After all, here is a man who is proven to be attractive to at least one other woman. So much so, that woman decided to dedicate her life to him.

Moreover, married men are perceived as being able to provide, protect and—ironically for philanderers—be more trustworthy than single men. Married men look like catches. Single women would not be contemplating relationships with them if they did not.

However, being involved with a taken man is a declaration to the Universe. It says you believe that you will never find love on a soul mate level. Another declaration is that there is something wrong with you and this all you can get. But the saddest declaration is that God has placed limitations on what he will give you, so you have to steal what you want instead.

All of those declarations are lies. You have got to be strong enough to be your own soul mate and walk away from temptation. You must have faith in yourself that you can live alone, if need be. And if a single man with good qualities comes your way, you must be confident enough to trust him to do the right thing.

EMOTIONAL DIVORCE

Even the best "savers" sometimes run short of money in the love account. This happens when both parties take a little emotional currency here and there without replenishing the balance. Shortages then occur.

Conflict ensues and both partners dig through the metaphorical couch for change. Neither one is equipped to deal with the issues, expecting the other one to solve the problem. Both draw up "Will Work for Love" signs that they hold over their faces, blocking their beloved from view. Neither of them thinks about putting the signs down. Not being able to see through to the other side, the pair disconnects and loses hope.

Understand that soul mates sometimes draw faulty conclusions about what having a good relationship really means. They can have the idea that if you don't have impeccable happiness all the time, you don't have a good relationship. In other words, they wrongly believe that if love is real, happiness is automatic, impeccable, and foolproof.

But in reality, no one can make anyone else happy. We can only choose to offer our goodness to others, and we make this choice over and over again.

Long-term soul mates in overall satisfying relationships know this, even when troubling issues surface. However, if both parties are withholding goodness, issues can cause a relationship to become fragile or even shattered. During these times of frustration, the relationship is tested, and sometimes emotional divorces occur.

Periodic breaks should be considered normal—part of human nature—and never culminate in actual legal divorces. They are temporary emotional separations caused by a myriad of factors, great and small. Some causes are financial problems, unresolved frustration, over-focus on the children, sexual issues, boredom, and simply not growing together as a couple.

These contrary situations serve a purpose, though. As long as the conflict doesn't totally devolve into hell and both partners still desire reconciliation, emotional divorces can lead to a better relationship. Psychological and emotional growth often comes from unpleasant stimulation, and that stimulation stems from contradiction.

Consequently, even in soul mate relationships, arguments happen, accompanied by blameful accusations and tears. That's when we can feel like our most precious values and dreams aren't being supported by our mates. We feel rejected. We feel misunderstood. We feel fractured. This is a lonely and disheartening place to be.

Weeks and sometimes months may be needed to get to a better "couples" space. During the emotional divorce, both soul mates should work on their separate and shared issues and conquer them. No one has to move out during an emotional divorce. In fact, day-to-day life can carry on as usual. They just have to keep their eyes on the goal. The goal is not to seek a conflict-less relationship but to become developed enough to handle conflict while rebuilding trust.

Think of it this way. Emotional divorces are comparable to strenuous workouts. Just like the body replaces damaged muscle fibers in order to gain mass and strength, emotional divorces can replace hard feelings and misunderstandings with passionate affection, humility, and enlightenment.

Eventually, a soul mate grows enough to become more tolerant of their partner's faults and admit their own. The committed couple moves through the gridlock and goes on to recapture the spirits of trust and love, which are also both active choices. They will learn not to allow the negatives of the relationship to take control of their bodies, minds, and spirits; instead, they will choose to cultivate the positives.

New conditions (boundaries) will likely be set. Any paranoia or unfounded worries must be done away with, too. However, unconditional love most likely will be strengthened. And the resultant reaffirmation of unity is the natural effect of the willingness to work through anger, hurt, and resentment. This can forge an unbreakable bond that is so powerful that it can be considered food for the soul.

THE MEANING OF WORDS

"I love you."

We say that little phrase many times a day. But how many times do we say it with passion and deep conviction? Is it just an offhanded way to say goodbye? Other times, do we say it just because someone said it to us?

Saying "I love you" is almost an autopilot response. Moreover, we've gotten to the point where we say we love everything. We love new pairs of shoes. We love the latest television show. We love slices of hot apple pie. The word "love" is in danger of becoming meaningless.

Let's start a new paradigm. This paradigm will change how we think of and express love. Love will not be just some commonly spoken word. We'll stop merely saying "I love you." Instead, we'll say, "I am going to *SHOW* you love, right now" and then get to it. Immediately, we'll give heartfelt hugs or kisses. We'll acknowledge our partner's contributions with genuine compliments. We'll offer much needed help to our lovers, especially when they are too proud to ask for it.

But if you really must verbally express love, say something that many don't. Tell your beloved, "I like you."

Like? Really?

Love is often dutiful affection or obligatory feelings toward someone rather than liking them. Moreover, love is an action word that we have to choose to do many times throughout the relationship. Whether love is a feeling or action, it requires maturity, and maturity requires effort.

And, unfortunately for some, love is equal to pain and suffering.

Love is not always about joy but *like* is. When you tell someone you like them, you let them know you are fond of them and desire to be in their presence. When you like someone, you actually feel good when you're with them. You feel joy…not pleasure but true joy. The combination of love and like takes a relationship to a whole other level. Mind you, that this kind of feeling is not only limited to soul mate love; you can have it for anyone you care for.

Liking someone isn't always easy. In fact, it can be more elusive than love. For example, think of your curmudgeon uncle. You know, the one who argues with everyone at the Thanksgiving table. You love him, but he sure as heck is difficult to like.

Everybody has bad days, and on those days, your loved one can be a miserable wretch. It may take some effort but try to remember what you like about them. Is it their sense of humor? Brilliance? Compassion? Something about them fascinated and drew you in. If it's still there, focus on that.

Better yet, imagine how you'd feel if some other person took notice of the very thing you liked about your lover and now have difficulty seeing or take for granted.

Ah, I bet that changed your perspective.

In the end, soul mate "like" and "love" are what you make them. This liking and loving need constant care and attention to flourish, and that is as it should be. Your soul will not be satisfied with anything less than you and your partner becoming a united expression of God's love.

TWIN FLAMES: A REASON A SEASON, BUT NOT A LIFETIME

Though we've been discussing soul mates, there is another type of relationship to be aware of. See, somewhere out there is a person who will make you feel so good…so alive…that you'll be convinced they're your soul mate. There'll be something different about them, *and* you, when you're together. You'll start to breathe them, so much so that you need resuscitation when they are not there. You'll believe they are the beginning and ending of you.

However, despite the fated feeling, your relationship with them will have difficulty staying together. You'll be chasing them or vice versa. Every trite disagreement will seem to devolve into an epic battle of wills. Aching and bleeding hearts go beyond healing. Breakups are inevitable. Sometimes the parting is amicable, but most likely, one or both of you will be left brutally destroyed. You'll lament and be totally confused as to why something that felt so right didn't work out. But somehow, with a change of perspective, you'll miraculously look back on the encounter with gratitude for the blessing it bestowed.

These are the markings of a twin flame encounter.

Let me start by saying that people define the terms "twin flame" and "soul mate" in many different ways. For our purpose, we will distinguish a twin flame from a soul mate by (1) the people involved and (2) the purpose the relationship serves.

But before we delve into the differences, let's start with the one thing twin flames and soul mates have in common: both of them are nothing like "basic" relationships. Basic relationships are all about the superficial aspects of romantic love. They are the plain white t-shirts of the dating world. Just like white t-shirts, basic relationships are easy to get into and easily discarded. Infatuation, sex, and normal breakups are par for the course. Contrarily, soul mates and twin flames are like ridiculously expensive designer dress shirts. But one you wear to your corporate office; the other you wear to a funeral.

Let's now get to the differences. A soul mate pair consists of two *already* whole individuals. Both have mastered the art of being alone without being lonely. Though their quirks and personalities may differ from each other and the contrast is enjoyed, they tend to share core values that contribute to their relationship's longevity. Soul mates are far from perfect and aren't immune to upheavals and pain, but since both partners seek stability, they are somehow able to work through the hard times. This is because, as a unit, they are repelled by turmoil and disordered interaction. Soul mates never get a euphoric rush from pain. Rather, they prefer the *beauty* of steadiness.

Twin flames, on the other hand, come to teach a different lesson about love. They are sometimes emotionally unstable. Also, one (or both) is the catalyst for some sort of personal transformation. This type of transformation is a death of sorts. It is the death of a comfort zone—no matter how destructive that comfort zone may be. Therefore, dealing with a twin flame is one of the most expedient ways to ascend to a higher psychological and spiritual state.

Passion is what brings twin flames together; however, it's not the addictive love-high of superficial romantic or sexually driven passion. The fervor twin flames induce is the kind that makes us walk a tightrope.

Twin flame relationships are passionately driven by their otherworldly intensity. That feverish intensity is what makes it so terribly difficult to differentiate between the soul mate and the twin flame. The twin flame feels like a peculiar blend of an extraordinary romance and soul mate. In fact, a twin flame relationship can rival the depth of a soul mate one. Twin flame-type relationships need that intensity because, if we knew the hard lessons and the transformation slated to take place, we would avoid them right from the start. When it comes to twin flames, there is going to be crisis. There is going to be running away. There is going to be a goodbye.

Why do we attract these twin flames in the first place?

There are often rogue aspects of our minds or outer lives that we choose to ignore. We need to change but don't know how to go about it. Subconsciously, we seek out a metaphoric death experience because we need to die to be reborn. That's when our twin flames show up. More likely than not, at first, they seem like dreams come true. Often, they appear as our "types" but can come in other forms. But no matter their presentations, our encounters with them are different than ordinary love affairs.

At some point, our twin flames expose very specific wants and fears hiding inside us. Essentially, they act like matches that light the fuses for life bombs, and most bombs are lit to destroy something. After detonation, we are forced to deal with those rogue aspects of our minds and outer lives that keep us in bondage. Indeed, twin flames have the ability to uncannily bring to light our private horrors. Whatever is lacking or what we have buried, our twin flames lay bare.

These same issues are energetic and have *already* been seeking exposure on their own. Somehow, some way, they have managed to manifest themselves in the material realm. They showed up as money problems, clinginess, unresolved issues from an abusive childhood, or whatever else we're running from. But we constantly dismissed them.

Bear in mind that the material world is just the representation of mental, emotional, or spiritual concepts. Take money, for instance. Let's say you've been ignoring personal money problems. And here comes your twin flame. If your twin flame has to give you money or *takes it*, what do you think money represents to you on different levels? When you look at material matters abstractly, you can see more clearly what your twin flame is really about.

However, twin flame relationships don't get right to the point; they never initially reveal why they have come into our lives. Twin flame relationships like to be drawn out, taking their time to burn down all our escape routes.

Moreover, the true purpose of the twin flame relationship can play out against the backdrop of some other drama. This drama may be overt or subtly tension filled. We'll think problems with our twin flame are about one thing, when they're actually about something else lurking under the surface. That is why the relationship always seems to be heading away from the real problem.

Eventually, a pattern will be noticed when the same issues keep popping up. We'll also notice that we probably had the same problem in the past with other people. This is when we have to ask hard questions of ourselves like: Is it really about their cheating or is it because of our lack of self-love? Did the twin flame come along to give us a chance to get rid of self-rejection?

Once we understand the big why behind all the little whys, then we can receive the gift of wisdom. Wisdom will force us to be honest and change. The changing won't be easy, because if it was, we wouldn't have needed to experience the twin flame.

During our ascendance, our egos will try to convince us that we can live with missing parts of our soul and our efforts to change won't be worth it. Egos will also tempt us to cling tighter to our twin flames because they seem to be the keepers of the very thing, or the change, we need.

But if we keep at it, we do learn how to detach and let go, not only from our twin flames but also the internal chaos that brought them to us. There is *beauty* in that. That beauty teaches us about the majesty of painful metamorphosis, grief, and letting go. But most importantly, it makes us recover our soul mate relationship with ourselves. Twin flames actually prepare us to love our soul mates with more honest hearts. That resultant love is fuller and deeper because of hard lessons we had to learn. Most importantly, they make us recover our soul relationship with ourselves. We should express gratitude toward our twin flames for that.

IT BEARS REPEATING

The love of soul mates doesn't only show up when everything is copacetic. The purity of their love really reveals itself during those difficult times when it seems easier to walk away. Trust is built in the trenches—when accountability and consciously loving another person carries more weight. It takes selflessness and sheer will power. This is why falling in love is so much easier than staying in love.

Affirmations are repeated declarations that turn into reality— *the essence of the declaration, that is.* The essence (the true intention/ the why) fueling the affirmation will find some way to come into existence, no matter what our mouths say. For instance, repeating "I am my own perfect soul mate" has the potential to penetrate and take hold of our minds. If the desire is pure, *and* it aligns with our true intention, so it will be. But sometimes after we declare an affirmation to "date" ourselves, something's off. We still aren't content with being with ourselves. Upon closer inspection, we discover our affirmations are really lip service, and we're just going through the motions. The essence of what we *truly* want is operating, and what we want is an external love, the demi-god who we think will make the sun shine and the moon glow. We can't manifest being our own soul mate while pining for someone else.

In that case, we are unaware that our untamed egos are working hard to maintain control. Egos are lonely entities. They are terrified of us separating from them and fully becoming one with our souls. They need us to believe that we are not enough, that someone else should be responsible for our emotional lives. When our egos seem to be getting the best of us, this is a good time to pull out a pen and sheet of paper.

Write down the qualities of your ideal soul mate by asking the Five Ws (who, what, when, where and why) in present tense: *Who* is he? *What* loving things is he or she doing for me? *When* are they showing love to me? *Where* do they show their love to me? *Why* are they loving me?

After you answer the Ws, make a simple change—change the "he or she is" phrases to "I am." For example, for *WHO*, change "He is courageous" to "I am courageous." Place the paper where it can be seen throughout the day. And don't just look at the Ws; do and be them. Every loving act will be like a drop of love in a cup that can be sipped on whenever soul thirst occurs.

But no matter how lofty we get, there is always the possibility that someone will have a magnetizing effect on us. Remember, the soul draws to it the people it chooses to experience. But even if those magnificent people leave us—or never even show up—we are never truly alone. If our souls have allowed other people to come, they're just there to help us remember who we are.

Regardless of who is or is not there, we are all awesome. Therefore, we must invest in ourselves because we always take care of what we honor.

SOUL AFFIRMATION

My soul mate is a symbol of my spiritual relationship with God. Even though I am already complete, my soul mate shows me unrecognized, undiscovered, or underdeveloped parts of myself. My soul mate is not limited to one person, though. My soul mate can be found in the faces of many. But to experience that wonderful connection, I just need to find one person. But even if I never find that person, I can rest assured that my soul is mated to God always.

CHAPTER 7

SOUL SISTER

People who need help sometimes
look a lot like people who don't need help.

—Glennon Doyle

As an individual, you are in the process of becoming a soul sister. This is your *singular* journey to become a better version of yourself. However, our soul sisters are friends who we fully experience life with. Sometimes we can feel closer to these women than our families because they accept, understand, and respect us more than some blood relatives.

There is not a single path to friendship. Just like the winter sky creates unique snowflakes, women create friendships through a variety of ways. But no matter what kind of friendships women share, a true sisterhood will always be based on some sort of commonality. This common bond will be the base that sets the tone and tenor for friendship—basically, defining its purpose.

NOT JUST SOME CHICK

As God's children, we are all connected to each other by His spirit. This connection works itself out through our varied relationships, including friendship.

In a spiritual sense, our friends can be seen as compressed versions of different aspects of the infinite God. With this in mind, the ingenious way God's spirit brings our universal connection into our awareness through friendship—a form of sisterhood—is quite beautiful and fascinating. Through His divine wisdom, He saw fit to give us options as to *how* a friendship could develop. Some friends are congenital, developing by happenstance, stemming from our inherited backgrounds. Others are willful choices. But some seem to be handpicked by God Himself, and these are the ones that have the most profound effect on us. No matter how we become friends, God is always operating behind the scenes. This is because He needs a way to experience His *own* love and that is through us.

It all started at our creation. During the first stages of our emotional development, God set it up so that our very lives depended on the connections we made. Women lived in small tribes and were usually kin, one way or another. While the menfolk were out mastering their hunting skills, the women stayed behind. As they cooked and made clothes, they shared laughter, regaled each other with stories to pass the time, and gave each other support. These were our first models for friendship.

Fast-forward a few millennia. It's still true that our first friends come from our relatives, like our cousins or younger aunts. These genetic tribal friends are usually the first group we learn to socialize with. Since these are our relatives, these friends are unique because of their genetic similarity to us. They often share the memories of our ancestors, passed through genetics. These blood ties are real and contribute to psychic bonding. Familial friendships are the gateway into more complex ones because they give us our first relationship lessons in a secure environment.

But since we are no longer primitive people and can't only associate with our kinfolk, we have to grow. Indeed, God still works in the modern world, and He mandates strangers' souls to evolve and grow into soul sisters together. So, He inspires us to go out and willfully choose women to be our friends.

Just the act of seeking friendship means that we want to have sisters, not only with family but others. If soul sisterhood could be defined only by that, any woman could be our sister. But that's not true. Many women have acquaintances and hangout buddies but no soul sisters. Soul sisters are wholly different.

It doesn't matter where a soul sister's friends come from, they are bound by DNA. If her friend is her kin, the DNA is familial (biological or legal). But outside of the family, this DNA is *mental* and *spiritual*. Regardless of DNA type, the strands consist of the sense of family that she gives and receives from her friends. Therefore, a soul sister considers her friends to be her emotional and psychological breed. A soul sister feels familiar and comfortable. We can relax with her because she knows where we are coming from, and there is no need to explain "what it's like."

You are acting like a soul sister when you want to touch your friend at the deepest level of her being. But you have to know yourself first and only enter that friendship after you've done some soul searching by asking questions: Who's the real me? What talents and gifts do I have? Who can I share that with wholeheartedly?

Then after you've felt the God-connection between you and a friend, it is your duty as a soul sister to be humble. Be thankful that someone allowed you to be privy to her private self—her real self. Defenses down, it is up to you to be humble enough to give her the best you have. And because it's a soul friendship, you won't mind because your friend is *not just some chick*.

The God connection between soul friends, a.k.a. soul sisters, is always fully operational. Every encounter with your friend will be special because God's love is exchanged. This is the mechanism by which two women go from mere acquaintances to soul sisters. As a result, any barriers between you and your soul sister are brought down. Both of you can be your most authentic selves. Your specific interests can be fully explored with a friend of like mind, no matter how bland or outrageous these interests are. Also, you and your soul sister can hold opposite views, giving you an exciting and challenging way to see life.

And guess what. As a soul sister, you don't have to limit your friendships to women you see every day. You can establish a tribal bond with unseen ones. Like fibers in a net, these connections can be through any humanitarian cause. Take the ones on social media, for example. Each fiber weaves together and creates a net that catches all things positive. As you impact women you do not know, the net grows larger and stronger. Soon enough, the net has the strength to bear the weight of all the women involved, and its influence cannot be contained.

It doesn't matter where your soul sisters come from; origin is of no concern. What's important is that soul sisters are all about supporting and loving each other through the tremendous variance of highs and lows that occur in life. These are the women that bravely take your hand and trudge through life's sticky muck when no one else is willing or able to do it.

But no matter what form your soul sisters take, ideally, these friendships should be of the highest nature and have much variety. Dealing with lofty and contrasting soul sisters will make you a well-rounded individual. You will have enough variety and differing points of view to make your life more flavorful.

Most of all, your soul sisters will teach you about your humanity. You will learn about acceptance, boundaries, and patience. Other lessons will include giving/receiving and embracing/letting go. But behind all the lessons is the knowledge of how the greatness of God's spirit ties us all together.

JUDDER

So, we've explored the concept of tribes as it relates to friendship. Let's go a little further, get a little mystical even, and get into vibration. Vibration is a psychological and spiritual frequency that falls on a spectrum ranging from low to high. High vibration energies consist of positive thoughts. Thoughts of forgiveness, optimism, courage, harmony, love, and reverence for life are all examples of high vibrations. Higher thoughts cause our spiritual light to vibrate and radiate a vibrant aura. Low vibration, however, results from focusing on the negative. Fear, rage, regret, and hopelessness all cause a fall into low vibrational patterns. The spiritual light becomes dim and cloudy, *though a fascinating personality can disguise this and fool other people.*

We are born with neutral vibrations. But our childhoods, youthful life experiences, society-at-large, and our reaction to those things slides our vibration toward one end of the spectrum or the other. After years of habitually entertaining certain thoughts and behaviors, our minds and bodies can settle at that vibration.

Everyone is always in the process of doing one of three things: creating new circumstances, maintaining circumstances, or destroying circumstances—either positively or negatively. Our internal radars ping on people who are doing the same things we are, generally. Their vibration tends to be the same as ours, and we want to make friends with them.

The quickest way to ascertain a potential friend's vibe is to simply look at the results of her life. This is not a foolproof method of judgment, absolutely not guaranteed, but it can be pretty accurate. So, when considering whether or not you want to be friends with someone, first look at her life. Then ask yourself, *Do I want to be like her?*

That question is important because vibrations are like viruses. And viruses have range, a sphere of influence. For example, your frequency may be blue. You may be a pure blue or have more yellow or red added. Those combinations allow for the movement between blue, green or purple. That is what is meant by range.

You can catch your friend's vibrational range. In other words, whatever range your friend is operating on, you will rise or fall to the same. That is why people of the same frequencies but different ranges, if they are in the same proximity or have contact with each other over a long enough period of time, eventually meld.

Typically, the women we select to be our soul sisters are a high vibrational match to us. But not all of the women we call friends vibrate at a high level, yet we still are drawn to them. To explain this, let's refer back to the previous chapter. Just like there is a difference between a soul mate and a twin flame when it comes to our sisterhoods, there is a difference between a high vibrational match and someone we are attracted to.

A kind of strange "Law of Attraction" is at work when we are irresistibly drawn to another woman and become her friend, even though one or both of us is operating at a very low frequency. Things start out great, but a singular or series of triggering events expose that someone has some type of negativity that needs to be purged. Without self-reflection, one of you can't see the truth and will instead blame herself for choosing the other as a friend.

But remember, God is at work and that attraction you felt was part of an exquisite "bigger" plan. The built-in triggering event was a catalyst for some lesson. Either you or your friend needed a prompt. One of you is the learner (pain receiver), while the other one is the teacher (pain giver). This pain takes many forms such as gossip, rejection, backstabbing, unreliability, etc. Regardless of the pain's form, the teacher is subconsciously driven to deliver it. The lesson is rarely easy, and it can be hard to understand the pain giver's motivation when seen from a mundane perspective. Moreover, when friends are dealing with the aftermath of the trigger, usually neither is thinking, *Wow, this is an awesome learning experience. Whoo Hoo!*

When the evitable triggering event occurs, and if you happen to be the friend who receives the pain, try not to fixate on the fallout.

Focus on the fall *UP*. Get the lesson, grow from it so that you don't have to go through the lesson again, and have yourself a good laugh.

Is that easy to do that? Heck, no. And honestly, unless one has evolved, laughing at unpleasant experiences most likely won't happen right away. But it is possible and that is dependent on your level of vibration.

Surely, you want to have high vibration friends in your life. Therefore, you're going to have to be honest. Take a look at your own vibration. Think about those areas of your life that you vibrate high and the ones you could improve. Also, consider if the friends in your life right now are vibrating high in areas that you are already high in? Are they vibrating high in the areas you want to improve? Their success or failure will rub off on you.

That brings us to the friend who is operating at a *super* vibration. This vibration is born out of fire. A fire friend is a woman who has been through hell, came through to the other side, and learned that even the most searing burns aren't fatal. A fire vibration is the result of being broken down to a cellular level and taking the last bit of soul strength you have and building yourself back up. A fire friend's purpose is to reveal that falling apart is really just reassembly and that sometimes we have to let go of what is loved too much. She also teaches us how to say "thank you" to the Universe when all things precious have been taken away.

The "thank you" is for the gift of being forced to REALLY go there. "There" meaning a realm removed from normal human consciousness and was the only place for her to escape to when earthly circumstances buried her. Not many people get to see that realm. Most don't want to.

But this is alchemy, turning poison into the cure.

Fire friends are the ones who bring you back to life when you are in despair, not just with pep talks or money but with a true spiritual infusion that you can only get from going "there." On a larger scale, a fire friend is a friend to all. She is that ONE…the one able to literally speak magic to crowds or bring life to the spiritually dead.

But privately, these fire-filled women are often alone. Many don't have a lot of friends. The fire within them is so great that it can incite either too much love or too much fear in others. However, the ones that properly love them are ready for the magnitude, and sometimes the severity, of the fire friend's journey. The other ones aren't ready for the intense waves of vibrations that hit the soul like a gong.

However, fire friends aren't superior to other friends. Not all of us are meant to rattle the ether with a super vibration. God creates balance by equipping all of us to handle certain levels of vibrations because we have *different* purposes. Most of us have less intense purposes because life isn't intended to be serious all the time. That's why girlfriends who are all about light and sunshine—especially if they are truly of a high vibration—are so vital.

So, whether our friendships are breezy and full of cheer or vehicles for trauma recovery and transformation, neither is better or worse. Regardless of which type of friendships we find ourselves in, it is best to keep them at the highest vibration possible and use them to bring light into the world.

THE BLINDING LIGHT OF MANY SUNS

Those high vibrations have to be put to practical use. However, we typically can't do that effectively until we gain the wisdom of experience that allows us to evolve toward our highest natures. And sometimes it seems like we'll never get there because our transformations are never-ending.

The good news is that one of the quickest ways to evolve—to gain a higher vibration—is to help another woman evolve. It works because our spiritual DNA is linked, and as one rises or falls, so does the other. It is sublimely altruistic and justifiably selfish to keep your soul sister's and your spirits up. Admittedly, the development and sharing of a high vibration looks erudite on paper. But that's not going to help you in real life unless you know how to demonstrate certain principles. Those principles can be summed up in one word: *empowerment*.

Empowerment is the harnessing and ability to transfer the light of God. God's light is the power and force that causes something greater to be created through higher vibrational thoughts and actions. It is dormant until someone harnesses and shares it with a gracious receiver. In turn, that receiver returns it or shares the light with someone else.

Considering women have this incredible light inside of them, it's no wonder why we are potentially powerful beyond belief. But sadly, we can be afraid of working together because of petty differences and strife. For example, women often hold other women to higher standards than men. Women oftentimes forgive men's grievous sins but will doggedly hold other women accountable for small infractions.

If women want to truly empower one another, we need to value and honor each other as if we ARE each other. And to do that, we need to make a permanent shift from a *me-mind* to a *we-mind*. We can begin by empowering women emotionally, because at its most basic level, empowerment is relating to our soul sisters with sincere feelings. We share the same heart, acquired from the accumulation of similar life experiences. These experiences have made us able to relate to different women, not only with sympathy but with true empathy. We don't only have textbook or theoretical knowledge about another woman's life. As soul sisters, we have lived it, too; we all had *something*.

That something took us down to the darkest part of our souls and made us doubt life itself. However, our times of sorrow taught us that our looks, money in the bank, who our spouses are, or our professions mean nothing when the bad times come. Now we can accept and use the light of God to overcome whatever problems come our way. We earned insight.

Insight gives you the ability to see when your sister has put her feet on the wrong path. Though you may be able to see her misguided choice, you may be reluctant to speak out. But insight lets you know that complicit silence is enabling. Because you truly love her, you'll be able to use insight and summon the light of God as your strength. You'll no longer be motivated by fear and are ready to meet her resistance. The light inside of you will push you to keep the pressure on her to be accountable. It's not about judgment, but when your soul sister is in trouble, you have to let her know she's messing up and empower her to do better.

Empowerment is not all about heavy emotional support and tough love, though. Part of empowering our soul sisters is filling them up with the absolute joy of living. We are to embolden our soul sisters with our optimistic outlook and hope, no matter what they've been through. After all, when people feel good, they are more apt to be kind and generous to others. It's a win for everybody.

We can spread light by simply smiling and seeing the beauty of every soul sister we come in contact with. And despite any heartache and pain they've experienced, we help them understand the advantages of growing and changing from those experiences. As their frequencies rise, they become happier and go about raising the frequencies of other women. Hence, a positive feedback loop is created.

High-frequency, empowered women stay on the dayside of emotions. The higher our frequency, the more we can sniff out a gloomy or dysfunctional person and maintain a safe distance. Fated lessons and strange Law of Attraction relationships aside, to consciously choose a dysfunctional woman as a friend means we'd be volunteering to be dragged down into despair with her, and that is not something anyone should do. That is truly disempowering for everyone involved.

Instead, when we are empowered and empowering someone else, we know that every second is a new beginning and a chance to create a space filled with happy, bright people. If a soul sister has temporarily fallen on hard times or is learning a strenuous spiritual lesson, we can empower her with a bit of our own happiness and light. Conversely, if she is in a great place, we can be empowered by her.

But let's keep in mind that the joy we're speaking about is genuine, not contrived. Only real joy can empower. So, we have to make sure that we are the real-est women in the room. No fronts are allowed if we are endeavoring to empower others. We can't be afraid to open up about our insecurities and fears. We have to be okay with being vulnerable and admitting that our life is not perfect. This kind of honesty requires trust based on proven loyalty. It's impossible to empower or be empowered in an ambiguous situation. But the onus is on the empowering one. If we desire to empower, we've got to prove that we are forever faithful, and our word is our bond. We should always be willing to disregard any selfish interests in favor of building a dedicated relationship. We have to show that we can always be counted on to give time, energy, affection, and even money if a genuine need arose.

However, we are not here to be patsies, and our loyalty is at first given but then has to be maintained. In other words, our initial loyalty is an investment in the relationship and comes with the reasonable expectation of loyalty in return. If your efforts to empower another woman aren't appreciated, don't hesitate to cut her loose from your life. That's called empowering yourself.

Indeed, empowering yourself may be the best way to empower others. When we are powerful, we inspire other women to mirror us. That's because as we create the best versions of ourselves, we infuse the air with life. The atmosphere practically crackles with our electricity, and our auras are attractive when we act as uplifting examples of living life to the fullest. We can do this, even if we have to publicly address an embarrassing personal or professional issue. Though those particular situations are tough, as empowered women, we own up to our mistakes, make amends if need be, and move forward in a positive manner. As a result, we become examples of grace under fire and inspiring reference points for fellow soul sisters who may go through a similar tough time.

But we can't do any of the wonderfully empowering things we've talked about unless we are present with our soul sisters, in the here and now. Generally, we are taught to be future-oriented. However, that mental disposition is not conducive for the formation of empowering friendships. When it comes to empowering our soul sisters, we should try to make time stand still. Our minds should not be jumping through time, thinking about the night's laundry, future hair appointments, children's recitals, mentally writing out business reports for the next day, or focusing on any other distraction. When we are with our soul sisters, we should just be present and give our full attention to the phenomenal human beings in front of us.

Sometimes being present can be overwhelming, especially if your soul sister is going through a difficult time. You may be afraid of what she's going through or drained by it. Reactions like those are normal. But because she is your soul sister and you love her, you have to draw on your own reserves and give the gift of your presence to her. Sometimes people don't need you to do a task or say the right thing; they just need you to be there.

And as you empower that one soul sister with God's light, she'll heal and empower another. Pretty soon, the world is bathing in the blinding light of many suns.

COMPETITION

Ah, competitive friends. For some of you, competition and friendship are two words that should never go together. You may think competition between friends brings down vibrations and is disempowering. But that wouldn't be accurate because sometimes our best friends are our most stiff competition.

Unfortunately, competition amongst women gets a bad rap. It's seen mostly in a negative context—the greater person wins; the lesser person loses. But competition itself is not only good; it's also natural.

As humans, we constantly compete to have our needs met, especially higher order ones. Examples of these are security, love, social acceptance, achievement, and self-actualization. Yes, even these lofty ideals require some degree of competition to achieve, depending on the evolutionary level of the individual. With that said, it's proper to set goals because that is one of the ways we grow as human beings, and it's also okay to have amiable contests with people we care about. For example, you can practice-race against a girlfriend to prepare for a marathon.

Friendly contests prepare you for the sphere of real and intense competition. However, competitors are not only external. You'll always have an internal competition going on as your constantly-burgeoning new self competes for dominance against your old self. This is your biggest competition. You are to strive to be better than you were yesterday. Life is about understanding that losses will occur, but at the same time, you have to be grateful for challenges.

Nevertheless, women are sometimes at a disadvantage regarding competition when compared to their male peers. For the most part, men are hardwired for competition and are socialized for it. Hence, they generally know how to compete and compete well. They don't take the game too personally and are lauded by society for their competitive spirits.

Though times have changed, women are still seen as less feminine or bitchy if they have a competitive spirit, especially if they compete with men. When women compete against each other, the competition often is over men, looks, children's achievements, and material assets. That is why some women insist that they don't compete with one another because what they compete for can be so petty. As a result, the air of competition around women can reek like spoiled halibut on a dirty sock. This is especially bad when the ruinous competition is between friends. This type of unhealthy competition can turn a friend into a frenemy, and the competitors can't tell the difference between normal and destructive competition.

Normal competition is driven by inspiration. Inspiration generates enthusiasm, creativity, and noble actions. There are no hard feelings or undermining. This positive competition allows a worthy competitor (our friend) to show us how to do better and not be embittered by her success. As a result, we avoid becoming envious of each other's skills and talents; we aspire toward them instead. For example, if there are areas that you are successful in, yet your friend lags, some friendly competition could help her hone her latent skills. Likewise, inspirational competition is a good measuring stick to help you measure your progress or come to the realization that your talents might lie elsewhere. However, inspirational competition can result in a wonderful blending of talents as you realize that the two of you have equal but differing abilities that can be utilized by both parties. Lastly, inspirational competition teaches friends how to succeed graciously and lose convivially to the other.

Contrarily, destructive competition is driven by inflation. This would be the inflation of the self-serving ego. The ego can only compete by being lower-minded and motivated by fear. It can never see a win-win situation; it can only see winner-take-all. There is no prize in equality; the ego has to have more than the other. This is its only measure of success. To achieve its prize, the ego entices the competitor to resort to mind games or shady tactics to win. All while smiling, the ego-driven one tries to subvert her friend's efforts and sabotage her achievements by backstabbing, lying, hogging the spotlight, and other ruthless behavior. Also, the underhanded competitor experiences *Schadenfreude* whenever her friend fails in her endeavors, especially if the underhanded competitor wanted the same thing. *Glückschmerz*, however, can cause the unscrupulous friend to have actual physical pain when she sees her friend win or achieve a goal.

The crux of the matter is that the cagey friend is seeking happiness that's not based on real achievement. She only can compare, believes there is not enough to go around, and wants human favor over God's. This emptiness can consume her soul and psyche. And the saddest part is that the unfriendly competitor may think she is still being a buddy as long as she is going through the other motions of friendship.

However, soul sisterhood is nothing like that. Soul sisters have discernment about the two types of competition. They gravitate toward inspirational competition and use its passion to achieve greater things. Mutual grace and humility act as their guideposts.

Soul sisters embody the spirits of cooperation and fair play to empower not only their own worthwhile goals but others' goals as well. This sportsmanship is not only directed toward our girlfriends but also to other people we compete with.

Now, just because everyone feels empowered, it does *not* mean that there are no losers, all participants receive a trophy, or everyone gets the job. That defeats the purpose of competition and leads to apathy. What it does mean is that our attitudes about competition are realistic, reflect humility, and give everyone opportunity. Those attitudes stop a soul sister from one-upping her girlfriends. She knows that life has its seasons, with all of its sunshine and storms. And like life, people have their time to excel and be on top; but sometimes they must walk in someone else's shadow. During those times when a soul sister is witnessing her friend's accomplishments, she is not brooding with jealousy. The soul sister is doing the complete opposite. She is loudly rejoicing and calling attention to her friend's success. After all, the soul sister would want the same kindness.

But that same soul sister feels sorrow when her friend didn't get her prize. She is right there giving love, sensitivity, and laughter to uplift the mood. Acting as a refuge, she helps her friend by being a temporary buffer from more pain. The soul sister is all about taking the journey together, forging an unbreakable bond that lifts her friend's soul to a more peaceful place in the midst of failure. Doing this, both friends always win in some way. The dignity, respect, and integrity they share are all rewards.

I CAN SEE RIGHT THROUGH YOU

There must be transparency for friendships to thrive. Transparency is basically open communication. It promotes trust and emotional security between friends while encouraging both parties to be accountable for the condition of the relationship. Moreover, transparency greatly increases the ability to share kindness and generosity because suspicion is decreased.

Transparency also gives friends the gift of being able to share their struggles without fear of judgment. When soul sisterhood is coupled with transparency, girlfriends can finally relax, knowing that the other one is not wearing some sort of personality costume that could be flung off during their most vulnerable moments.

Let's start with truthfulness. Opinion is often mistaken for the truth and is always biased. For example, statistics are often really opinions set to numbers. People often use "statistics" to prove their points of view. However, those statistical numbers usually are gathered and presented in a way that looks like factual data, but the research material is cherry-picked and manipulated to serve the researcher or the funder of the project.

Truth is being real about what is going on in an effort to create the highest good. This is where compassion comes in. A friend can be blunt about a situation, thinking she is telling the truth. But she is really blurting out a hurtful opinion based on her own experience and prejudice. However, an honest friend knows how to deliver an uncomfortable truth in a measured, compassionate way. We have to be open with each other and avoid omission where facts must be revealed. And we have to be willing to accept rejection if what we say is beneficial, but the receiver does not want to hear it. Our friends have their own versions of the reality, and those perspectives are just as valid as ours.

We're all imperfect; therefore, nitpicking does nothing to enhance the quality of a soul sisterhood. Make it a point not to hyper-focus on inconsequential things and concentrate on the more positive attributes of your girlfriend.

Privacy is also a helpful. Some people may believe that transparency means that everything should be out in the open. It is the freedom to be who you are while not unnecessarily disclosing certain aspects of your external life or internal world to other people. Essentially, if what you are doing does not hurt anyone or is *no longer* relevant, you can keep it to yourself.

With all that said, transparency has another quality—it allows light to come through. This light is spread when we take accountability, love generously, and remove ego-driven desires. We become "trust conduits" and allow trust to flow from one soul sister to another. Trust gives us the chance to not only enjoy our friendships, but we can also share in each other's burdens without feeling smothered.

Ultimately, we should strive to be true-to-the-core friends who will *always* be there and help our girls carry their burdens. Our job is to stay calm long enough for them to refocus and put their minds back on a Higher Power. Fortunately, most of the time, it is not that serious, and we can just enjoy each other's company.

SOUL AFFIRMATION

Some of my friends came from the same womb. Other friends came to me through serendipity or when one of us was deep in heartache. In spite of everything, I love my friends with all my heart. I pledge to be there when they need me, celebrate their victories, and lend an ear when no one else will listen. That is the least I can do for such great people.

CHAPTER 8

THE SOUL OF MOTHERHOOD

*There is no greater burden on a child than
the unlived life of a parent.*

—Carl Jung

You won't know the greatest sacrifice, the ultimate fear, the protector in you, or the feeling that surpasses even love…until you become a mother.

Motherhood is often portrayed as a perpetual pink and blue dream. But any woman who has ever endeavored to be a mother knows motherhood is nothing but trench work. Motherhood is one of the toughest, yet most fulfilling, roles we play as women and is also one of the most unappreciated, even by us.

Whether you are a stay-at-home mom or have a career outside the home, raising our children is not only an honor but a duty to mankind. Of course, there are those days when we feel like *"Ugh! Is this even worth it?"* and the option of locking ourselves in the bathroom away from the kids looks pretty good. But those are the times we have to remind ourselves that motherhood is doing God's work. As women, we must come to terms with our phenomenal power to change the world, and one of the ways we can achieve that is through our children. Therefore, the purpose of motherhood is to improve the world by raising children to be positive, functioning adults who contribute to society. It takes a lot of effort to raise a future generation that is more intelligent, moral, and peace-driven than we are. We are building exceptional men and women, indeed. If we screw that up, we are in big trouble.

Think of mothering as an assembly line project of sorts. Mothering is assembling the best parts of ourselves and putting them into a new creation. And that is what we will be talking about in this chapter—the parts. But before we get into the parts, we've got to talk about the parts maker.

BREATHING YOUR OWN AIR

When our children are born, we are not only cradling infants in our arms, we are holding potential. As we coo at our little bundles, we can't help but to fast-forward to their first days of school, learning to ride bikes, and proms. Before our babies leave the hospital, we are already so proud of the possibility of who they might become and who we will be in relation to that.

But as time goes on and reality sets in, this wishful thinking can develop into an unhealthy fixation. Like Pinocchio, our unfulfilled dreams want to become real children. These are the dreams we tried to achieve but failed; or if we didn't have the skills, courage, or knowledge to pursue, these are the desires we suppressed.

Sometimes our physical children may have a natural inclination for things that interest us. However, there may be instances when we may gently nudge or even forcibly push our children toward our unmet goals and desires when their wills are too young to say no. Accommodating, sensitive children will dutifully try to please parents. They may develop stress and suffer guilt if they fall short. More independent children will mature and eventually rebel, sometimes fiercely, against molds they don't want to fit.

Soul moms understand that children are not vehicles for wish fulfillment, and that in order to raise whole, competent children, we must breathe our own air. We must embody whatever characteristics we find admirable and not depend on our children to do it for us.

That brings us to the void. The void is an inner longing, a psychic nagging-ness, that tells us we are less than...that we are missing something. If there is a void, we must go inside ourselves to examine it and figure out its cause. When we understand our own void and do the work of filling it, we can authentically enjoy our children's victories and achievements without the interference of our self-aggrandizing egos taking credit for it.

Initially, we should not strive to fill the void with things or activities. Those are secondary. First, the void must be filled with wisdom and the realization of God within us. Then we have to have an idea of what we really want and why we want it. This is the tricky part because we can be addicted to concrete form rather than essence.

It's the essence that we desire. Essence is the *feeling* we want to experience when we obtain the "form." That feeling is what drives us. Once the desired feeling is discovered, we have to look at our present lives and see the areas where we already have that feeling. When we do this, we're able to see just how close to or far away from our external goals we are.

Now, what are some of those feelings, those essences, we are looking for?

The most basic yet beneficial feeling we seek is love, specifically self-love. It all starts here because if you don't have self-love, you will "suck the air" from someone else. Self-love is imperative in the development of our own soul. It's about nurturing ourselves. We have to eradicate covetousness of others' beauty, money, intelligence or anything that belongs to someone else. Also, we must not lust after false praise and instead desire our own validation.

The next feeling we seek is peace. We all want to have freedom, and peace is freedom. It is freedom from fear, shame, stagnant struggle, and conflict. We can facilitate peace by using the simple yet profound act of forgiveness of others and ourselves.

Another feeling that we want is confidence. Confidence is having faith that God is watching out for us and also that we can achieve great things. Hence, confidence doesn't originate from external sources, like people telling us how amazing we are. Indeed, it feels good when someone gives us credit. However, praise can be like a drug...the more you have, the more you need the effect. Too much praise becomes redundant and ends up losing all its meaning. Therefore, we must temper our enjoyment of praise with a humble spirit by taking it lightly because one day we won't be on top. And that is the day we will be confident enough to say, "Well, it wasn't my time to shine," and go on with our lives.

Another sought after feeling is joy. The best joy comes from appreciating another person's joy. There are so many blessings in that alone. It is a profound recognition that we are all one and their good is ours also. We also obtain joy by giving it to others. It's just as easy to spread happiness as it is to spread misery. One leads to expansion; the other leads to despair. We always have a choice. And again, we have to remember that what we give to others, we give to ourselves.

Lastly, we want the feeling of release. Release is basically letting go of damaging emotions, particularly anger. This is critical because many mothers are unable to process their anger properly. They carry pain around and use it to lash out at the world, oftentimes in front of their children. However, being slow to anger and quick to let it go are ways to unknot the soul. Release frees our children, too; because being as sensitive as they are, they can actually feel it when our hearts are light.

Life will not always give us what we want, and therein lies the void. Inspirational feelings that fill the void are God-given, but we must embrace them. When we breathe our own air by maximizing our positive feelings, it is amazing how much better we feel. No, we won't achieve every goal we reach for, and the airless void is always tempting us. But it is how we deal with the void that matters. We can go a long way to keep our voids filled, so that we don't look to our children to do so.

Now, take a breath.

THE FIRST TEACHER

Since we're breathing on our own now, it's time to rub our palms together and get into those "parts" of motherhood.

Mothering is another word for teaching. Our classrooms extend beyond the walls of our homes. Wherever we are, our children are learning how to interact with us and the world. Though our sage advice is helpful, it is really our actions children learn from the most. Therefore, it is imperative that we are living examples of dignity, optimism, helpfulness, grace, and even zaniness.

But some parts (aspects of humanity) require a more formal approach. Regarding these, observation may not be enough; they need to be laid out in an instructional manner with lots of sit-down talks:

POSITIVE THINKING

Just like adults, children have to master the art of positive thinking. This is especially true since children have more active imaginations that can make them perceive more difficulty than there actually is. Teens are especially prone to catastrophic thinking. Everything is an emergency or something that will make them feel as though their life is over.

The first step in positive thinking is listening to the negative self-talk without fear. Fearlessness will help the child determine if the self-talk is really negative or their soul urging them to learn from and correct errors. Mothers need to be honest about the inner critic because defeatist thoughts plague all of us at one time or another. This should be done in an age-appropriate way.

Listening to, but not being consumed by, negative self-talk is valuable because it provides a way for unpleasant feelings to be expressed and released rather than suppressed. However, negative self-talk should be handled with caution as not to promote guilt, anxiety, or compound an already negative self-image.

After the negative-self talk has been dealt with, a child should be encouraged to make a list of what they like about themselves and their accomplishments. This is like a palate cleanser after being exposed to and letting go of negative self-talk. Display this list prominently where the child can see it frequently. The child now has a clearer idea of what's good about her. This will result in increased confidence and inspire her to try new things.

But here is a special tip. Whenever your child is caught in a whirl of negative thoughts, suggest that the child smiles. This mind-body connection will result in an elevated feeling and will enhance her ability to find creative solutions to her present problem.

Sometimes children just have to be taught to take a leap of faith and move forward rather than staying stuck in the revolving door of negativity. As they make their way toward a beneficial outcome, their souls replenish, filling up with light and positivity, which helps them become awesome people. This can be tough, but when we have trained our children properly, they have the courage of their convictions to lean on.

RESILIENCE

No one is immune to the problems and tragedies of life, including our children. That is why it is imperative to teach them resilience. Resilience is the ability to continue on in life after a setback or disappointment while learning a valuable life lesson in the process.

The most resilient of us have developed methods to meet challenges head-on without buckling. These are called coping skills. Coping skills help to reduce stress and this allows children to more effectively handle difficult situations. The child who has learned positive coping skills knows how to find an alternate solution when their original plan doesn't work out.

Coping skills are highly individualized; what works for one child may not work for another. You and your child may have to explore several to see which one works the best. Fortunately, there are endless ways to cope with stressful situations. Maintaining an optimistic attitude is an extremely beneficial coping skill. Talking about feelings helps with the release of anxiety instead of internalizing. Also, meditation or prayer helps to work through problems by helping the child listen to the inner voice. But one of the most effective coping skills is to help someone else. This gives a different perspective through the fruits of generosity.

With the use of coping skills, children develop resilience and are able transmute difficulties. Adversity breeds wisdom, and through it, children learn that handling tough situations with grace, perseverance, and strength turns into a gift. So, when times get tough for our little ones, we have to remember that character is only built and revealed during hard times. We start teaching this lesson to our kids when they are young; even toddlers can get that lesson.

BEING A PART OF THE GREATER HUMANITY

One of the truly wonderful things happening is that the younger generation is more global in their thinking. We have brought up children with mindsets that embrace everything that makes mankind unique. They are imbued with a rather special life skill: how to be contributing citizens of the world by serving others rather than the self.

But we must not rest, believing that there is nothing more to do. We must continue the good works we and our children do. There are many ways to do this. We keep up the message that all humans are our children's equals, and someone's character should be assessed according to their individual actions. Moreover, if someone is lacking in life's essentials such as food, clothing, shelter, and education, we should all be encouraged to help in any way we can.

Plus, we teach our children that nothing good has ever come from those who seek to divide, are cruel, react with violence in word or deed, or espouse any kind of hate, no matter how they try to slant or disguise it.

ETHICS

Sometimes children might perceive the right choice as the wrong choice. For instance, a youthful mind may think it's easier to cheat because they get the reward without the work and earning benefits over a period time may be seen as silly. Eventually, this thought process leads to the attitude that success or victory should be obtained at any costs, no matter who gets hurt in the process.

As mothers, we are to give our children ethics. The children, in turn, develop those ethics into their own moral codes. Children with moral codes have no use for illusory wins they did not attain with integrity. Of course, there will be times when children will not know the right choice to make, but we help them make decisions with conviction and pray for blessings in those choices. We impart the understanding that having the strength to do the right thing, even when it is hard, is empowering. Good choices are not always easy to make, so our children must hold fast to their faith through prayer, believing that God is all-knowing and to trust in Him.

DISCIPLINE

We have to love our children enough to discipline them. However, we shouldn't work from the premise that children are bad. Instead, we should "mother" with the idea that children come here to learn and grow, not only physically but mentally and spiritually as well. And part of that learning is that they can soar as high as eagles, but if they keep flying into walls, they will be grounded.

Discipline is boundary setting for children's learning and protection. Even though we strive to teach ethics and proper behavior to our children, kids will still be kids. They will inevitably overstep boundaries, backtalk, lie, and fight with their siblings. Though this behavior seems harmless, if left unchecked, it can escalate over the years. Next thing you know, a sullen, troublemaking teenager has sequestered himself in the bedroom down the hall. That is why it is up to us to help them understand that all actions, both good and bad, have consequences.

The concepts of being your kid's best friend or the "cool mom" should be tossed out the window. After all, they are minors living under your roof. Sure, you may second-guess your approach when it seems like all the neighborhood kids, including yours, want to hang out at the fun mom's house down the street. You may feel a sense of rejection and loneliness because of your decision to maintain discipline and structure. But remember, to be that fun mom requires a grown woman to take on adolescent traits and that mentality is not conducive to order. The fun mom is usually the one who is too afraid to set real limits or discipline her kids when they step out of line.

No one is advocating you become a dampener. Enjoy your kids. *Have fun with them.* Just remember that children are our legacies, not accessories to help us retain our youth. It is up to us to use every tool at our disposal to help us raise our children and capitalize on all experiences to underscore the lessons we are teaching them… especially giving them consequences when they stray off the path.

But discipline in its purest sense is not about rules and regulations. It teaches the child to have self-love and how to self-regulate. And she will train herself to listen to her own consciousness rather than external forces.

COMMUNICATION

Children first learn how to communicate with their parents. Fortunately, most communication will be about mundane topics like what they did at school, dinner choices, or about the latest fashion trends. The point is to have an environment where the child feels safe enough to talk about anything.

Though general conversation may seem insignificant, it creates connections. Children will trust us as they joyfully and frightfully talk about life-shaping events, and how they affect them and their view of the world.

Our next task is to teach children to communicate with people outside the home. They should learn not to pass judgment or shut others out because of differing opinions. Moreover, they should be taught the importance of the proper use of body language and tone.

QUALITY TIME

Another one of those motherhood "parts" is quality time. Quality time may be a bit of a misnomer when it comes to kids. Often, quality time is seen as a specified block of time dedicated to doing something productive or entertaining with your child. The actual amount of this time seems not to be important; the performing of the activity is the focus. Even if you just spend thirty minutes doing something so-called meaningful, that should be enough. Right? Not necessarily.

Children do not need "quality" time. They need time, period… and massive amounts of it. Children are time hogs, especially if they are preschool age and under. Whether you are doing dishes, balancing the checkbook, or running errands, if your child is with you that is important. Because it is not the doing-ness that matters; it is having you in their physical presence that counts.

Part of raising healthy, happy children is creating stability, i.e., security. In the modern age, that has been defined in terms of finances. However, abundant time spent with your child offers emotional security that only you, or a regular caregiver who is invested emotionally in the child, can give.

Admittedly, finances are important. And somebody has to put a roof over the child's head and food on table. But what we are talking about is disposable time and an observation that postponing some of our ambitions or free time to be with our children can be seen as a reluctant sacrifice. For some, viewing our children through video cameras on our computers is a more pleasant alternative. However, wee ones don't care if we want to spend our entire weekend with our girlfriends, put in extra hours to acquire that corner office that we crave, or would rather sleep in. And maybe that is a good thing because no one can take a rain check on the time spent with their kids. Once it is gone, it is gone for good. And children really do grow up fast. It may be a bit of a juggling act, but we have to learn how to balance the time spent between our kids, spouse, and with ourselves.

With that said, we should all take every opportunity, as time and money permit, to have dinners around the family table, walks with our kids, do chores together, or just lounge in front of the television. Because it is highly doubtful that on our last days on this Earth, one of our regrets will be that we spent too much time with our children.

THE TEEN YEARS

If you have adult children, was it more painful raising teens or having wisdom teeth extracted? You may have to give that some serious contemplation. But seriously, the teen years can be more than a little bit turbulent.

Children can be frightened and confused by the dramatic physical changes puberty brings. The resultant appearance of breasts, body hair, menstruation, and skin eruptions may make children extremely uncomfortable in their own skin. That doesn't even include those vertical spurts and increases in bone and muscle mass that contribute to clumsiness, which also increases self-consciousness.

Also, teenage-hood usually arrives with a sudden change in behavior. Our normally pleasant children now want to challenge everything as they strive to become more independent. Not only is this distancing traumatic to us but to our children as well. But the anguish we all feel does not stop their hormones from doing the treacherous job of transforming them from children to adults.

However, no matter how much height children gain, or how much hair covers their bodies, they are not adults yet, and we still have to parent them. And who is in control may become a big issue. Teens' misbehavior is the result of the ensuing power struggle. As moms, we have to respond to behavioral problems by enforcing discipline, sometimes harshly.

None of us want to take on the bad cop role. But if circumstances arise, moms have to love their children more than themselves and their comfort zones. Moms have to be strong enough to take the pelts of stinging backtalk or morose pouting. Despite our best intentions, when on the receiving end of insolent behavior and the silent treatment, our hearts break and cause us to second-guess our decisions as we wonder how we may have contributed to the situation. Mommy guilt is real. The funny thing about it is that the guilt arises most when we are being a proper parent instead of a "liked" one.

We want our kids to think we are awesome and be our happy appendages. However, teens usually have other plans, and those plans include being selfish, rude, aggressive, or performing self-harming behaviors. So, we have to enforce the rules. Yet when we do, it can be difficult not to succumb to the illusion that our willful teens are still tots. We see their cherubic faces and our resistance evaporates. Our hearts and minds want to revert to the role of protector instead of disciplinarian. We want to coddle instead of imposing rules.

If not dealt with quickly, mommy guilt has serious consequences. It can make us waffle on the rules, so there is confusion as to what is expected from our children. Also, mommy guilt can encourage us to become too lenient in an effort to win back the affection of our teens.

The cycle starts with the teen doing something wrong over and over again. Then the teen is constantly rewarded for it because parents seek approval from the teen rather than risk confrontation and alienation. The teen is emboldened by the goodness he/she receives and keeps up the disruptive behavior. He/she may start to act out toward other family members, peer group, or even through their own self-sabotage.

Fortunately, our warrior souls can be summoned for strength. Warrior souls remind us that our job is not to be our children's friends; it is to be mothers, bound with the responsibility of molding our children into functioning adults. And when children balk at our management style, we must let them know that the real world is much harder and tougher than we are, and children have to be prepared for it.

But no matter how good we try to be, parenting a teen is exhausting. There will be many days where conflict will not be resolved, and we will have to go to bed with no clue what to do next. Those are the times we will feel like utter failures, even with our warrior souls cheering us on. But with time and practice, we learn, forgive ourselves, and move forward. We don't have to be perfect, but we can be effective by using tough love. Tough love has to be tempered with reason and the gradual granting of privileges in direct proportion to maturity level displayed by the child. Coupled with tough love, shared wisdom helps children navigate the tumult of their teen years. They may grumble when we offer advice or at our tough tone, but they really are listening.

But most of all, we are giving our children chances to live in the fleeting and wondrous moments of their teen years. And we should try to enjoy those years, too. The teen years are really an exciting and amazing time. At the end of our children's transformations, we get to finally see who our children *really* are.

BULLYING

One of the most disconcerting issues today is bullying. It is a bulldozer used to tear down a child's budding self-esteem. Sadly, bullying is an effective weapon and is wielded often, not only in school but also social media. Bullied children, as a result, can be primed for depression. For some children, drugs and suicide seem like ways to escape. Others may seek revenge that results in great emotional or physical violence.

However, a bully often is not the terrible fiend we expect him to be. Sometimes a bully is a child who is crying out for attention, emulating his parents' behaviors, or experiencing some bullying or violence in his own life. As with most bullies, the child is really just trying to transfer his pain onto others. This action may work in the short term, but its ill effects are temporary, and the bully must resort to the same behavior again to have a release.

Now, if your child is being bullied, you have to step in immediately. If the bullying is occurring in a structured setting such as school or a sports team, a meeting with the administration or coach is required. If possible, the bully's parents should be there, too. If it is a neighbor's child, go to the parents and let them know what is going on. But before these steps are taken, your child must have some measure of psychological and physical protection in place. Of course, walking away from a bully is the best thing. However, some bullies are relentlessly provoking. So, it is best to speak to your child about how your family would handle certain matters, such as physical encounters, before they occur.

Also, as conscientious mothers, we have to be forever vigilant and watch out for signs that our own daughters aren't becoming domineering or our sons aren't resorting to force to get what they want.

OF GIRLS AND BOYS

Despite living in the age of sexual equality, male and female children still face different circumstances and challenges.

Girls are now taught to compete more than they ever have in the past. And they are mostly competing with other girls. There is nothing wrong with positive competition. It forces young women to utilize their strengths and overcome their weaknesses. However, girls are generally not taught the art of *healthy* competition as much as boys. Boys, being more emotionally detached, compete and still remain friends or at least maintain some semblance of respect for one another.

But girls are more complex than boys. They add a lush emotional component to their intellect. That is why they can be more prone to tear another young woman down, not only to compete but to destroy her emotional strength.

Moms must teach their daughters that using emotional force is not the same as true strength, and that they will grow stronger as they build other girls and women up. Despite this teaching, there will probably come a time when other young ladies feel the desire to tear our daughters down.

When my daughter was bullied, I wanted to remind her how awesome she was because the acts of school bullies were devastating to her. I told her that when we do extraordinary things, people notice us, and their jealousy may make them act against us. I wanted her to know that she should never let this negative attention stop her from speaking her mind or being a leader. I told her that people who are insecure or jealous are immature in their reactions. I would tell her (1) the aggressor must really think you are awesome to expend so much energy on you, and that (2) it is the aggressor's own insecurities making them believe that by stomping on a beautiful soul, it will somehow build up their own. However, the truth of bullies is that my second point was more apt. I would never want her or any other young woman to believe that their actions created an abusive situation. We have to teach them that the only way to rise above the torment is to understand that it really is about the other person, not them.

Another area to be aware of is social media. So many young women unfairly compare themselves to the glossed-up images of their peers and celebrities online. They see illusions of perfection and then observe their own lives which are often perceived as drab by comparison. Conversely, the social media illusionists never expose their tricks: great lighting, artificial enhancement of photos, staging, and scouted locations. Both the spectator and performer participate in the fantasy, except one feels terrible and the other one makes a profit. With all the media pressure girls face to be popular, smart, pretty, and thin, it is so important to instill self-esteem at an early age.

This brings us to our sons. Moms must teach boys that great men live with humble hearts, knowing there is something bigger than them (namely God). Moreover, boys must be taught to accept life's rewards and gifts with a grateful heart while not holding on to fleeting things too tightly. As they grow older, we should help them become more confident in their ability to achieve anything they set their minds to, if it is in God's plan, and that any success in their lives is a direct result of God's help and our son's individual effort.

And just like we advocate sisterhood for our daughters, we must do the same regarding the joy of brotherhood for our boys. Our sons should be comfortable uplifting other moms' sons and inspiring them to be upstanding men. We do this by teaching them to be outstanding themselves and seeking that quality in their peer group. Together, our sons will become confident leaders and sometimes supportive followers.

Boys should also be allowed a space for them to acknowledge that they are not perfect and sometimes are afraid. We should reiterate to our male children that everyone is a work in progress and greatness comes from recognizing and overcoming our flaws. Also, let them know that fear is not a weakness but running away from challenges is.

It is also crucial that we teach our sons how to treat women with respect. Children model their parents' behavior. That means, as parents, our actions hold more weight than our words, but they should be used together. This symbiosis is inevitably melded in the brains of our sons. For example, as moms, we tell our children we love them all the time. However, if we did not perform the action of love, our children would have no idea what love meant. Moreover, the father should express his love verbally to the mother; but love in action takes precedence over words. Therefore, if we want our boys to properly care about women, it is the parents' job to create healthy, respectful environments where unselfish love is displayed.

Piggybacking on the role of the adult male, moms should also make sure the men in our sons' lives are good role models. The men should be caring toward the mothers but also teach the boys how to be confident as men. There is such a fine line between being confident and arrogant. Arrogance is self-importance, possessing a superiority complex (which is actually an inferiority complex turned inside out), and an ego dedicated to serving the self. Arrogance spills over into all areas of life, especially personal relationships.

However, if the mother and father aren't together, both should be mature and responsible enough to show respect toward each other.

Moms, single or married, need to be acutely aware of the type of treatment they are willing to accept from men. Just like a young girl will form her relationship patterns based on her relationship with her father, a son will treat a woman the way he sees his mother being treated. If we allow ourselves to be treated horribly by the men in our lives, our sons will subconsciously get the message that is acceptable behavior and may treat other women in the same manner.

Our behaviors—conscious and unconscious—mold the actions of our male and female children. Children are impressionable, psychic sponges if you will, who pick up on nuances from the parents about how to treat, perceive, and talk to the opposite sex. Boys and girls are body language experts.

Sometimes a mother laments over why her child (male or female) has gotten in trouble with the opposite sex. The mother defends herself by saying, "I did not teach them to act like that." But upon closer examination, even though she never verbally expressed something, her unconscious-driven actions did, and the child picked them up and mirrored them back.

This is not mother-blaming, but we are talking strictly about soul-type motherhood. Fathers will have to write their own book.

THE VILLAGE

No matter how much we mothers create nurturing spaces within the confines of our homes, the cold world still waits right outside our door. Yes, we wish, hope, and pray that our children will embody the lessons we've taught them, and that the world will make an exception by welcoming them with hugs and kisses. However, as soon as our children's feet step on the porch, they discover that the world is not always kind and makes quick work of assailing them with ideas and values contradictory to what they've learned from us. Literally, the best we can do for our children is the best we can do, and we have to trust that our wisdom is strong within them. Letting our children go…well…this calls for faith.

Faith is magnetizing. It draws to us other mothers whose fingers are also pulling away from their children's hands. Like us, these mothers' hunger to create the proverbial village that raises children and protects them when they leave their "first" homes. As we meet each other, one by one, our village grows into a community of like-minded mothers who see all children as their own. It doesn't matter how we come together, just as long as we find a way to connect.

As villagers, we all have a reason to ensure that every mother's child does well. And that is daunting because of the world's hypnotic allure which encourages bad behavior. Though individually we may not have been able to do it, the village can counterbalance the influential weight of this realm. The villagers realize, ultimately, it's not only individual families raising children; communities raise children, too.

But our village is not only concerned about children; it's also responsive to all its mothers' needs. Every well-run village knows that if mothers are in distress, the children can't blossom. By taking care of the village's life bearers, the community offers weary and confused moms "life" gifts, particularly forgiveness.

Forgiveness is simply grace given at this moment. See, we can't hop in a time machine to go back and fix the mistakes we made as we were learning how to raise our children. We carry around so much guilt because we can't mend the past. Fortunately, the village is a place filled with caring and thoughtful mothers who inspire each other to wipe out their soul-numbing mommy guilt. After all, we should've

never strived to be perfect because that wasn't going to happen…
and never will. Instead, we should be given a chance to recognize our
errors as learning opportunities and move on with no regrets.

Sure, mothering the future generation has its trying moments,
even under the best of circumstances. But when we stand together
—strong and proud—positive change and growth always occur, not
only in our village but also the world. Then as we grow older, our children take the helm. They start over with their own children, carrying
forward our triumphs and correcting our mistakes.

Soon enough, we'll be living in our children's village. That's
why it is so vitally important to pray every night for other mothers
who have difficulty finding peace in the midst of the chaos going
on around them. Their children will grow up and be the keepers of
the new village, too. Therefore, praying for other mothers' and their
children's peace is really praying for ourselves.

However, praying for other moms and their children is just the
first step. The next one is getting out there and doing something
for them. Slogans and head nods don't get the job done. We are all
sisters and have to put in the work by *actively* supporting each other.
Carpooling, babysitting, and volunteering at school are some ways
we can help other mothers.

Sometimes, though, we will be called to help a mother who has
more pressing concerns. That mother may even be part of a large
community of troubled mothers who need not only physical help,
but someone to look past the sludge of their situations and see them
as the daughters of God that they really are.

But no matter how small or big the challenges may be, as dedicated
mothers, we can create this village. And we *have* to do it because we are
in this together. It is through all of our children that we create a heaven
on earth.

SOUL AFFIRMATION

I invest in my child and use all sorts of currency. I give my money, time, emotions, and spirit. I give because I am investing in my child's immediate needs and future greatness. But I do this not only for my child but also for other mothers' children. Whatever I put in helps my child and other children rise. Therefore, my giving is truly the best investment I can make.

CHAPTER 9

THE SOUL OF A DAUGHTER

We honor our parents by carrying their best forward and laying the rest down. By fighting and taming the demons that laid them low and now reside in us.

—Bruce Springsteen

No matter how old we get, we are still someone's child. Even as we take on careers, mortgages, marriages, and children of our own, there is still part of us that wants to be our parents' baby. So, it comes as no surprise that we think our parents should still dedicate their golden years to us and their grandchildren (extensions of us). This could create problems in our relationship dynamic when our middle-aged and elderly parents' needs and desires conflict with ours.

This is because we, as adults, can have arrested development. During our formative years, parents provide our basic needs and offer emotional support. But when we reach adulthood, the relationship becomes symbiotic, and we are expected to carry half of it. The responsibility for maintaining the relationship now has to flow in two directions.

Some of us, however, still feel it is necessary to carry childish behavior into our adult relationship with our parents. Any unresolved differences from childhood, entitlement issues, or just rude behavior are the results of this. Moreover, our parents may want to enjoy their lives, filling their time with new hobbies and interests that don't include us, and if we are clingy, our parents' newfound freedom is not likely to go over well.

Life transitions can bring out conflicts of interests and power struggles. The parent may seek to exert control by reinforcing their dominant role, or they may simply disengage by making themselves less available physically and/or emotionally. The adult child, on the other hand, can resort to manipulation tactics. They may suddenly become helpless and require rescue. Other times, they may manipulate with guilt that forces the parent to prove their love and loyalty.

Both sides can avoid these unfortunate outcomes by maintaining and strengthening the familial bond. Outpouring of affection, affirming communication, and demonstrable trust are ways bonds are reinforced. Parents and children must make these actions priorities. Sometimes the effort is not made because it is assumed that the familial link can't be broken. Nothing should be taken for granted, however. And we have to learn to be fully aware of the strong and sometimes tenuous bonds we share with our parents.

Sometimes those bonds are hard to maintain because of resentment. But we have to be willing to have sympathy and empathy for our parents. When we understand that they, too, are mere humans, we can see them more clearly. Though our parents love us, they couldn't teach knowledge that they didn't have nor could they behave in ways that they were not taught. This is not excusing any behavior; this is reacting toward them with love, in particular, *agape* love. *Agape* love is not the common feel-good type of love. *Agape* love is transcendent because it always exists regardless of circumstances.

PERPETUAL WOMB

We can sometimes have difficulties when it comes to being adult daughters. Unresolved baggage from childhood is often to blame. We are consciously aware of some of this baggage. This propels us to capture something we didn't get as a child, such as unconditional love, or we work to overcome the ill effects of something we didn't want but got anyway, such as abuse.

Not all childhood issues are obvious, though. Most of the time, we struggle with a more subtle psychic disturbance. It's a nebulous, haunting feeling of emptiness called hesitant independence. Some of its symptoms are laziness, childish emotions, and a fear of being alone.

See, it doesn't matter how old we are; we still long for the comfy shelter of our mothers' wombs. But that does not negate the fact that mentally healthy adults strive for independence (which makes them feel secure within themselves) and ownership of their lives.

But maybe we came from homes where we were never taught to stand on our own, relish the strength of womanhood, or were only shown love when we were in crisis. In these cases, as we evolve from child to adult, we can be ambivalent about being independent. Part of us wants to be a child, innocent and free. Then there is another part that wants to sever all dependent ties and strike out on its own; but for whatever reason, it can't seem to do it.

Even if we were raised in homes that taught self-reliance, the world can still be frightening. At some time or another, we all wish we were *in utero* again. We may even try to achieve some semblance of this by unwittingly falling back on dependent patterns from childhood. These patterns can take many forms such as using parents as financial crutches, relying on them to enable our emotional weaknesses, and making them the scapegoats for our failures. These are simply tricks we employ to re-enter the womb.

Exposing our desire to remain dependent is not meant to induce guilt. In fact, it's a normal response to want to give our unwanted baggage to someone else, in this case, our parents. It's also normal to desire undying love, which is usually sourced by our parents, in particularly our mothers. We can't help but want to feel innocent and loved. However, it goes deeper than even that.

Love them or "hate" them, our parents are like God to us. We came forth from their bodies and they nurtured us, for better or worse, and we always crave their love. But as we grow older, we discover that the natural progression of life will prevent us from having that forevermore with them. This can throw us into a crisis, a feeling that we always lose what we have. And that is scary. But the reason for this crisis is not on the surface; it is hidden. Yet we feel the fear nonetheless. To assuage the fear, our unconscious starts to think, *maybe my dependency will keep my parents with me forever.*

There are many triggers for crises involving our perception of losing our parents, but we will focus on two. The first is a parent's blossoming love life. Our antennas can rise when our never-married or divorced parental figures bring new lovers into the fold. This is especially true if the parent has postponed dating while we were growing up.

It would seem like our parents' romantic relationships would not affect us. After all, we are adults who span the ages of roughly eighteen to eighty, probable ages that our parents are still with us. But the transition can be harsh for those too dependent on the status quo.

Rarely do we see our parents as other than just mom or dad. However, despite our blinders, our parents are still sexual beings that crave romantic love and companionship. Hence, this may result in a serious dating relationship or even marriage. Our parents' new love interests can cause anger, resentment, and insecurities to rise out of our subconscious. The lovers become threats rather than being seen as enriching our lives, just as they would if we were juveniles. When that happens, it's impossible to form a bond with this new person.

The better way to deal with the parent's lover is to be accepting. A bond really can happen with this new person. After all, "parents" come in many forms: psychological, adoptive, and even spiritual.

The second crisis-trigger instills fear in even the bravest of us. This crisis has two parts: illness and aging. Few of us grew up with an ailing parent. Mostly, when we reflect back on our childhoods, we remember our parental figures as young and vibrant human beings. As we matured, we did not pay too much attention to the fact that our caretakers were growing older, too.

Then one day, we are full-fledged adults and may notice some changes our parents are undergoing, but we ignore it. However, as our parents enter into their middle and elder years, psychological, spiritual, and physical changes can overwhelm them, with the physical being the most challenging. Aging can bring on a range of problems like minor aches and pains to debilitating illness. If the latter happens, our formerly independent parents will depend on us to be their caretakers.

Most of the time, we are unprepared for the role reversal. And usually, this switch happens at an inopportune time, when we have so much to juggle to keep our own lives in check. The stress of not only taking care of our children but also our households, careers, social interests, and romantic relationships can make us feel over-burdened.

Moreover, it's terrifying to see our parents in a frail state and a sense of helplessness can prevail. It can be soul-crushing to lose the support that our parents gave us because they simply can no longer do it. Add to that the financial considerations for medication, doctors, and hospitalizations. We may also experience heightened conflict with siblings over delivery of care and who is responsible for what: some do too much; some do too little.

In the end, all the battles and depression we may experience stem from one of our worst fears—losing a parent. The inevitable aging and possible illness of our parents makes this a stark reality, and we just don't want to deal with that notion. We want our parents back, back to the way they used to be. Back to being our forevermore.

So, let's redirect our focus back to the womb. When all of our efforts to stay in the womb fail, we may unconsciously force our parents to baby us, even when they are sick. We set up situations where our parents have to come to our emotional or material rescue. For example, we reignite sibling rivalries by twisting situations and forcing our parents to take sides. If they are ill, we curl up in their beds but have them stroke us instead. Or we simply guilt them only so our weak sense of personhood is strengthened. Our manipulations can be so subtle that it's often difficult for us to see that we are the primary source of our fear.

Parents often just give in to our demands for attention. We, in turn, receive our reward—security of the parental womb—an illusion. It has now been proven to us that the way to gain safety and receive love is through the use of coercion and weakness. This can result in a never-ending cycle of manipulation-reward behavior.

But sometimes parents grow tired of being manipulated. As their intolerance grows, our neediness has less of an effect. Parents may reach a point where they tell us that they've done all they can and that we have to grow up, not only chronologically but also mentally and emotionally.

This is when the change comes. But we're the ones who have to change, not them. And no, it doesn't matter if they weren't what they should've been or what we craved them to be because, we're moving on from that. Indeed, we are to take a big gulp of that pride and swallow it. It's now time to actualize the person we should've naturally evolved into.

We start by questioning the ego's point of view and then rejecting the insecurities it thrusts upon us. As we separate our souls from the ego, we begin to accept and give forgiveness. And that includes forgiving everything. Self-forgiveness is recognizing that our actions were hurtful and making a promise not to do those things again. We have to forgive our parents, too. Forgiveness is not absolution. It's simply releasing the grip that pain has on us, setting everyone free in the process.

Next, we have to relinquish our fear of taking adult responsibilities. One responsibility we have is to love ourselves. When we love ourselves, we don't place an undue burden on others to give love to us.

And lastly, because time waits for no one, we must cherish every moment we have with our parents. True, everything is impermanent, but we can't live fearfully from that space. We accept life cycles for what they are. But in the meantime, we must love our parents with gusto, even if the situation demands that we love them from afar. However, if we can tolerate being in the same room with our parents, there will be no regrets over the time gifted to the ones who gave us life. If we can't find anything else to be thankful toward them for, it should at least be that.

THE MARVELOUS DAUGHTER

As soul women, we choose to take over some of our parents' duties and be the new foundation of the extended family. Though we may want to climb back into the metaphorical womb, we take on the challenge to embody certain traits so that we can lift burdens off our parents in their later years. Our new duties are:

Acting like an adult: We should see ourselves as independent beings. We stop being emotionally dependent and don't see our parents' actions as part of our identity. However, we still advocate for a mutually loving environment with no unrealistic attachment to past slights.

Understanding that our parents still love us despite their choices: We let our parents have the time and space to pursue their lives and just be who they are. If they are in a new romance or marriage, we peacefully let them have their relationship.

Avoiding ultimatums and threats: We don't make our parents choose between us and their choices.

Wanting the same happiness for our parents that we want for ourselves: Happiness spreads and is good for everybody.

Extending generosity to our parents: We should be thankful for the sacrifices our parents made for us and gladly give them blessings in return. Our kindness can come in many forms such as time, care, material assets, or a simple thank you. But no matter the form, it should come from the heart.

Maintaining healthy communication channels: A simple phone call to Mom and Dad can make their day. Keep most conversations light and lively. But some of those talks will address more serious issues. During those more somber talks, remember to be humane. And do your best to end the talk with love.

Honoring and respecting our parents: We should always avoid being rude, condescending, or just plain mean. Our parents deserve better than that, and we should be thankful for the time we have with them. Also, we should take advantage of opportunities to spend time with our parents. None of us know how much time we have left, so we must use it to spread as much love as we can. Even if our parents made mistakes, it is best to offer forgiveness and extend some understanding toward them while they're here. And if closure is the best option, offer them at least one heartfelt visit; loose ends can drive you mad. In the end, no one ever regrets the gift of time they gave to someone else.

THE BLESSINGS

The reality is that you are expected to properly adjust to your role as an adult child and understand it's not anyone else's responsibility to accommodate you. This goes whether you are a biological, step-, adoptive, or psychological child. Parents should be allowed their own happiness and peace.

Take the time to realize that it's truly a blessing to be someone's daughter. Physically, that means that we've had the opportunity to be given life through two people—our biological parents. And no matter the circumstances of our conceptions, we should be thankful for at least that. However, more importantly, we've been given spiritual and emotional opportunities as well. Spiritually, we're able to learn, grow, and change into the beings God created us to be. Emotionally, we get a chance to expand the idea of family. We get to love and be loved by not only our blood family but also anyone who we make a family with later on.

Finally, live your life as a tribute to your parents. Your actions should reflect dignity, grace, and a proper upbringing. Make good decisions and achieve admirable goals that your parents would be proud of. Be the type of daughter that makes people compliment your parents' ability to raise such a phenomenal woman.

SOUL AFFIRMATION

I am thankful for my parents. No matter what happened, I honor them for choosing to gift me with life. My relationship with them taught me so much about myself. As I grow older, becoming wiser day by day, I understand them more. I realize that for some of us, it is good to love our parents up close and personal. However, for others, it is best to love parents from afar. But regardless of distance, my prayers for my parents are not based on what they did for me. I pray for them because they are children of God, just as I am their child.

CHAPTER 10

SOUL FAMILY

There's a crack (or cracks) in everyone…
that's how the light of God gets in.

—Elizabeth Gilbert

In the twenty-first century, the definition of family has expanded. A family can now come in all sorts of configurations. The most common type of family consists of relatives. Relatives typically come through blood ties, while others are adopted or fostered. Another kind of family is one consisting of those people we have consciously chosen to be in our lives; these are matter-of-the-heart kindred. We are connected to them through the spirit and share the same wavelength. All of these types of families are usually celebrated. But there is another type of family that gets mixed reviews…the blended family.

Blended families usually consist of a couple with children from previous relationships. It must be noted, however, that people don't just bring children into marriages; they bring their whole clan: Momma, Daddy, Sister Marlene, Brother Timmy, Aunt Bertha, Cousin Leroy, and everybody else.

You may be saying to yourself that marriage, regardless of type, involves the coming together of two clans. However, blended families are different simply because of the children; the children are the differentiating factor.

It seems like societal shifts would make the formation and maintenance of blended families easier, that all parties would like to see a beneficial outcome. However, blended families often face unique challenges.

Before we begin, a clarification has to be made, and that is, no "type" of family is superior. Traditional nuclear families aren't immune to anger, heartache, betrayal, or any other negative situations and emotions.

But difficulties in blended families often arise from personality clashes. Hackles seem to be raised more easily because people can be more sensitive when they belong to a blended family. This is because before the formation of the new family, personalities have already been firmly set, and some family members would never have associated with each other if not for the marriage. After all, personality clashes with strangers on the street can be avoided, but that is hard to do at the family barbeque.

Fusion appears to be a major factor. In biological families, fusion is more likely, though not guaranteed. You're naturally inclined to become part of anything you're born into. However, in blended families, fusion can be a process because its members are expected to treat once-upon-a-time strangers as blood kin. Therefore, it is imperative to get a jump on potential pitfalls by educating and encouraging others to have a healthy idea about what the foundation of a family really is.

A family's foundation is not only founded on blood but also love and commitment. Actually, love and commitment take precedence over blood. Love and commitment make us more inclined to fuse. Fusion makes us love with our whole heart, whereas there may be times blood relations are conditional and require payback of some sort.

Now, if you are in a blended family situation where everything came together nicely, fantastic! You get a cookie. However, if you are about to enter into a new familial arrangement and unsure about it, this is valuable information that will at least prepare you, somewhat, as to what may lie ahead.

WHO ARE WE NOW?

Taylor. Jones. Smith. These common surnames, as well as infinite others, are used to bind us to our direct bloodlines and clans-at-large and help those outside our genetic loop to distinguish who we are. Moreover, names contain energy carried through time. Some names project themselves with strength and power. Others radiate more mental or spiritual qualities. Some exude softness or artisanal airs. Beyond the surname, families also have unconscious collective psyches which manifest as value systems and philosophies.

Families not only offer a sense of belonging but also identity. Identity is a challenge for blended families. The blended family is missing the cohesiveness of a blood tie, a tie that has not only a biological but also psychological and spiritual components. Biological families aren't perfect, but they often fall back on that blood tie to keep them together through all sorts of mayhem. So even though blended families have the capability to be more functional, they lack that blood tie. That's why they may need more attention and dedication to fill in the gap.

Another identity challenge is that while the parents are desirous of the merger, children may want to maintain the status quo. The children may feel that they have no choice in the matter and are at the mercy of the desires of the parents. In response, they may see a blended family as a threat to their autonomy and don't want to become an extension of a group not of their choosing.

These identity challenges should be met with understanding, not anger or resentment. Instead of wishing things were different, see blended families like random shards of glass coming together. If the edges are straight, smooth, and flat, the pieces can come together almost seamlessly. However, if the edges are rough and pointy, they may have a tremendously difficult time coming together. Spiky edges cut and hurt; if not compassionately dealt with, they lead to problems. Sometimes these problems come to the surface with breathtaking intensity. Other times, problems are sidestepped because of the fear of upsetting the already polarized participants.

The "who are we" of the family has to be defined. This will maintain the psychic unity called trust. Without trust, the foundation of love and commitment can't be laid. Vigilance is needed to maintain trust in the blended family. Vigilantly do whatever it takes to avoid the idea that blended families aren't valuable and are easy to toss away with the first hint of strife.

AXIS OF POWER

Every blended family has a central axis that maintains order, i.e., stability. Central axes have their own way of doing things. Some opt for the free-range approach, feeling that the setting of boundaries would be offensive or stifle familial progress. Others are hardliners, ruling with iron fists, feeling too much freedom would result in bedlam.

Could it be that both approaches are missing the mark? Too much leniency does indeed result in bedlam, and too much strictness is stifling. However, these polar-opposite approaches do have one thing in common: they are missing true leadership.

Superficially, the lenient and strict central axes seem to be acting the parts of leaders. But they are lacking true leadership because true leadership knows that respect does not come from over-yielding or strong-arming. Those are fear-based actions that make it seem as though power is externally derived from a willing or unwilling party. Therefore, either approach is really manipulation rather than leadership.

Also, it must be noted that central axes are formed before marriages begin. After the wedding bells have rung, the central axes continue to display true leadership work through their actions. These three actions are: generating faith, setting expectations, and enforcing the rules.

First, a central axis generates faith. Faith comes from the axis's proven ability to create a great family. Together, the couple builds this faith at the start of the new family by being patient, knowing that blending a family takes time and that everyone orients at their own pace. They understand that progress will be made some days, while on other days, family members revert back to old habits. However, under the central axis's direction, as long as everyone strives to be family oriented as opposed to self-oriented, everything eventually balances out.

Another way the central axis creates faith is encouraging an atmosphere where honest, non-combative communication can take place. The central axis doesn't take affronts personally. They know that everyone has moments of speaking without thinking. At the same time, they know when boundaries are overstepped. They immediately put a stop to it because they understand that cruel words spoken in a hateful way can take a long time to heal, if ever.

Faith is also created through service. Though there are many types of service, the central axis encourages service to the family. The central axis makes sure that all family members are serviced equally with love and respect. They encourage family members to help each other out, refusing to let petty disagreements and prideful arguments get in the way. Whenever the central axis receives help from the family, they boldly express gratitude by recognizing the abundance they receive.

The second action of true leadership is setting up expectations. People really do appreciate boundaries. No one thrives in madness. A lack of expectations is one of the top problems that all families have to deal with. But with blended families, the problem can be exacerbated. This is because blended family members can be splintered by having different agendas, and they can see the same scenario from vastly different perspectives. For example, when it comes to fights between stepsiblings, parents have a natural tendency to take their own child's side over a stepchild's. Frustration is made worse when children believe that a stepparent has no right to give them any discipline or directives whatsoever.

Expressing expectations before the marriage may not prevent future problems, but the family can be guided into having the same general outlook. The central axis must know each other's stance, especially on discipline and dealing with relatives. They must trust each other enough to get past the romance and take a business approach toward matters. A functioning central axis makes sure it agrees with each other's expectations and style of living. If they feel uncomfortable, they don't move forward as this may backfire. After much discussion, the central axis finds areas of agreement and builds on those. If there are any major differences of opinion, they can work those out before cementing the relationship.

The third action of leadership is to enforce the house rules that were created based on expectations. A central axis can have a meeting with relevant family members and explain these rules, making sure there are no gray areas that can be exploited later on. If the children are old enough, the central axis can draw up behavioral contracts for them to sign if potential problems are looming. For instance, a teen may claim that they do not "remember" a rule after they purposely break it. All the central axis has to do is pull out the contract with their signature on it. Obviously, a central axis doesn't want a police state; but they do want a well-run home. Their house rules make expectations and goals clear, not only for the children but the adults as well.

Regarding the enforcement of house rules, the central axis should always present a united front. That way, the likelihood of someone attempting a divide-and-conquer strategy will be lessened. However, there will always be those more strong-willed family members who will not think twice about pitting the central axis against each other, instigating awkward situations during the most inappropriate times or stoking lingering doubts and simmering tension already developing. Despite that, the united front shows who the real power in the home is. As the house rules are enforced, any manipulation, ultimatums, and bribery are put in check and given dire consequences. The central axis should never live in a hostage situation by handing over the soul of the marriage to other family members.

But what happens if the central axis doesn't forge a united front? In blended families, this sometimes happens when half of the axis believes that uniting with their spouse somehow means that they are aligning against their own family. The conflicted mate can't see that being in the axis doesn't automatically diminish their love for their own family, in particularly their children.

If the situation is not properly managed, house rules crumble because there will be no one to enforce them. The central axis will become adversaries instead of teammates. As the central axis's bond becomes more and more delicate, some family members may strike a fatal blow to the union. As the axis spars, they will never realize that the trouble didn't originate from them. Without knowing the genesis of the problem, they will be unable to solve it. The result will be the dissolution of not only the central axis but the blended family as well.

ANOTHER WAY TO LOOK AT IT

Blended families present us with a unique life-learning experience. Optimistic outlooks and dedicated efforts increase the probability of a successful merging. Family, after all, is only what you make it, and that holds true no matter what kind of family it is.

Finding the right balance can be daunting. But with time and diligence, our blended families can come together and enhance us in ways we never would've expected. They can teach us how to be patient and unconditional givers. They also teach us how to let things go. Ultimately, a blended family is just a soul family at its core.

Though genetic relatives are created through blood ties, a soul family is built on the foundations of choice, willingness to be open to love, and connectedness through the spirit of God. Simply put, the foundation of a soul family is that it came together *purposely*, to be a point where love, laughter, and home meet.

As we learn how to manage our blended families, we become more of the soul women we were meant to be. This is done by discovering skills, talents, and resolve that would've remained dormant if we had not encountered this situation. We should thank God for bringing these people into our lives. And when all goes well, we get to indulge in the radiant affection of those we **chose** to be our family.

Family, no matter what form it takes, is always built on a foundation of love, not blood. And, really, who couldn't use more love?

SOUL AFFIRMATION

I surrender to the process of building my blended family. I am flexible as I accept changes. I am also firm when my family needs my strength. I look forward to the exciting highs we will experience together, and I am prepared for the times when growing pains get the best of us. But even then, kindness, patience, and lots of humor will direct me as I guide my new kindred.

PART

—— 3 ——

**MIND + BODY + SOUL
= BEAUTIFUL**

CHAPTER 11

SWEET AND SOULFUL MIND

Beauty is how you feel inside, and it reflects in your eyes.
It is not something physical.

—Sophia Loren

People don't usually think of the mind as the starting point for health and beauty. Health and beauty are often thought of as things to be lived through the senses, while the mind doesn't physically exist, only its effects. After all, the mind can't be seen, heard, smelled, touched, or tasted. However, our minds—not our brains—are there, silently managing our lives. Thus, our minds determine our physical appearance and how we feel.

Though not physical, our minds require food in the form of thoughts, whether these thoughts are good or bad. Most thoughts just pop into our heads, and we usually don't question their validity, assuming they are true, especially those bad ones. Since most of our thoughts don't originate from a fully awakened state, where do they come from? They come from a particular level of consciousness.

For our purposes, we'll define three levels of consciousness as semi-awake, asleep, and comatose. These levels drive our actions, relapses, blocks, and default modes of being. They come about through cultural indoctrination, family conditioning, pain, and other external stimuli that impregnate us with someone else's reality.

Sensory-inducing stimuli and carefully crafted ideas conveyed through symbols, images, concepts, and word association are how foreign ideas etch into our minds. Negative impact moments called trauma also taint us. The perception and acceptance of these ideas and events—and also how our egos assign them a place in our lives—form the foundation of our personalities. As our personalities embody these concepts, they react with programmed responses that we think come from the "real" us. Without resistance, we accommodate assigned roles. We morph our thinking and bodies into what these roles are which reflect some kind of internal beauty/health or ugliness/sickness.

However, we can strive for more self-mastery by learning how to better manage our minds. We can then extract real beauty and vitality from our lives. So, let's examine the three consciousness levels (semi-awake, asleep, and comatose) and endeavor to regulate each one.

SEMI-AWAKE

Very few of us live in a fully awakened state, 24/7. Most of the time, we function at a semi-awake level. At the semi-awake level, we deal with everyday living. But the thing is, everyday living can be quite arduous.

In a world that demands instantaneous decisions, there is little time to contemplate or make clearheaded choices. We meet strangers every day and don't have a lot of time to figure out who they are. So, we rely on personalities, theirs and ours, to make snap judgments.

But instead of accurately accessing the situation, personalities are busy filtering the world, bending it to fit programmed perspectives. Generalizations and assumptions abound. And that's unfortunate because personalities think they are fully awake and know better. Through our personalities, we can only see what we can see. Consequently, many of our interactions are rife with confirmation bias, meaning we experience what our beliefs are.

We get so used to this mode of living that we can't even see what we are doing. We embrace our own stereotypes which are really nothing more than self-fulfilling prophecies. Imprinted labels prevent growth by denying our potential to be something else. Because we believe our own stereotypes, we assume others' stereotypes are true as well. We end up misjudging entire situations because of this.

But the good thing about the semi-awake level is that the negative behaviors we display aren't usually severe. Our issues are really just irritating personality "habits" that we fall back on when we aren't mindful. In fact, to some degree, we actually are already aware of these idiosyncrasies despite our programming, and we do wish to change.

However, there seems to be two semi-awake behavior patterns that are way too easy to embrace and stubbornly hold on to—toxic pride and perpetual victimhood. Toxic pride is the condition of having unwarranted self-importance. Its arrogance is deliciously enticing because everyone wants to feel special. But, when we are semi-awake, this specialness comes from unearned favor or assumed skills that have never been tested to see if we actually have them. That's why we like this specialness; we can feel proud for nothing.

Some of this stems from youth. Our parents tell us we are great simply because they love us. Dotingly, they clap and cheer for any little thing we do. However, some parents praised us for doing nothing at all. The younger we were when unearned praise and rewards were doled out, the more the ideas of specialness and "better" seared into our young minds.

Society-at-large blows up some of our heads even more with its teeming stereotypes about who is more special, beautiful, or the best. If we fit any of the descriptions, we rarely refuse the privileges.

The problem with toxic pride is that we will encounter someone who has actually been tried and tested. This person will demonstrate real worth through their deeds and achievements. Toxic pride, on the other hand, has removed opportunities for us to rise to challenges and be better instead of relying on the momentum of an image. Therefore, the falsity of toxic pride can't stand up to excellence's true owner.

If we do decide to achieve the idea of what others think we are, we have to humble our hearts. This is done by acknowledging that we may not be as superior as we think and give kudos to those who earned the right to claim a meaningful achievement. And then we do the actual work to become something that we can be genuinely proud of.

The next tightly held semi-awake behavior pattern is perpetual victimhood. It seems odd that anyone would choose to live from a state of never-ending victimhood. However, playing the part of a victim is quite effective.

On the surface, a perpetual victim speaks from total powerlessness. Yet, this powerlessness is strangely satisfying because of all the emotional support received. After all, there is a captive audience, especially people drawn to drama and pain, to testify to and gain attention from.

And like toxic pride, perpetual victimhood doesn't require effort. The victimizer is the action figure, and therefore the only one required to move forward by correction. The victim has the right to remain static, using the past as an excuse.

Perpetual victimhood also reveals a desire for revenge, seeking a demurely hostile solution by inciting another person to deliver punishment to the victimizer. This way the victim gets their revenge and simultaneously remains innocent.

Lastly, a perpetual victim holds power over someone by "guilting" them and demanding a limitless debt be paid.

This is not victim blaming, nor is it condoning evil acts. But a distinction has to be made between victim and victimhood. Victimhood is being *conscious* of a wrongdoing and choosing to stay in the pain and anger of it while that decision acts like a wrecking ball, destroying the possibility of a happy life. The woeful narrative repeated too often, never transmuted, or moved past, is a signal that someone is refusing to grab hold of the glorious beauty of living. The effects of this are: tarnished relationships for lack of forgiveness, rage that manifests as a disease that consumes the body, joy that can only come from pain, and a hardened heart that can no longer receive love.

ASLEEP

When we are at the asleep level, we have less mindfulness than we do when we are semi-awake. Being asleep causes suppression. We suppress any thought that takes us back to an awakened state, a state where we are fully conscious of unpleasant information.

Unlike the semi-awake level where we know we have adverse behaviors, when we are asleep, we make a very quick yet conscious choice not to be aware of our predicament. This choice happens fast, sometimes within a split second. We only become aware of what we've done after being triggered by a significant event or someone criticizes our behavior.

Triggers are our wakeup calls. Whenever we are triggered, we should investigate what we are feeling and why we are feeling those particular feelings. Then we should pay attention to what actions those feelings are inspiring us to do and how that worked for us in the past. If past actions had bad effects, we ask ourselves if we can let that negativity go. Next, we can choose other feelings we'd rather have...feelings like joy, bliss, peace, or courage...and then live from those. We can gradually release the negative mindset instead of going cold turkey. We do this by surrendering the old mindset little by little each day while simultaneously living out the mindset we would rather have. There's emotional safety in this approach.

Admittedly, a new mindset can be difficult to embody. It takes fortitude to "be" a new creature. For women, it can be especially tough. This is because most women want love and acceptance. But sometimes the acquisition of love and acceptance comes at a cost. Mental survival mechanisms and a desire for relationships can push us into an asleep state, because we make the decision to suppress our desire for a new mindset, a mindset that could threaten our connection with others—the sources of love and acceptance.

Our souls, however, demand that we develop positive selfhood. But in our efforts to secure acceptance and love, other people can see that same selfhood as a threat. Women who fully express their selfhood can be seen as the dreaded "too." Our being "too" is threatening to weaker-willed people…too strong, too smart, too independent, or too assertive. Punishment can be swift. Admonishment, shaming, slander, and isolation tactics are common.

Therefore, personalities and their egos believe they have to trick people so that they can get what they want. Although personalities are not our real selves, they make decisions for us. They decide how to get what we want through programmed behaviors. They go into our metaphorical closets and pull out one of four common suits that women typically wear to get what they want.

The first outfit is the coquette. When we put it on, we act girly and non-threatening. Our demeanor is crafted to give the appearance of a sunny attitude, always upbeat. But sometimes we feign fragility by using weaponized tears. The coquette gives us the ability to diminish ourselves, and that is its superpower.

But the flirtatious coquette can only go so far. Soon enough, we are at the mercy of the little girl persona, and the smallness looks like incompetency. Weaponized tears look like melodramatics. When we tire of wearing the coquette suit and put on another one, it may be too late because we still may not be taken seriously.

The next suit is the complaisant suit. In this suit, we are people pleasers, never wanting to cause any trouble. Even if someone behaves in a rude, slick manner toward us, we make excuses for them. We give absolution that we would not have gotten had the situation been reversed. Moreover, everyone else's desires supersede our own. We make others' dreams come true while ours turn into nightmares. But just like the coquette, removing the suit has consequences. People resent that we change up and become focused on our own needs instead of theirs, and we may be accused of being selfish.

Then there is the passive-aggressive suit. We wear this one when we have more willpower than the first two, but we are still very much aware that punishment awaits us if we appear to step out of line. So, we passive-aggressively fight. In a roundabout way, we confront or attack our perceived enemy. We pout, forget appointments, scheme behind the scenes, deliver low-key insults, or withhold critical information. No matter how non-aggressive we think we are, we are actually being quite destructive, brutal even. But despite our vicious behavior, we are still cowards. Indirect hostility reflects our fear of confronting obstacles directly and is a weakness.

Finally, there is the suit most people don't like seeing women wear—the aggressive suit. Let's be clear on something: *a woman wearing the aggressive suit is not the same as a soul warrior*. The aggressive suit is just that—a suit. It is a temporary accessory we don so that we can deal with frustrating situations, but we tend to be over-emotional in it. Conversely, a soul warrior does not go in and out of her being, fluxing. She is stable with her passion, dedicated to a cause, and uses her feistiness to accomplish goals, regardless of pushback.

Now, in the aggressive suit, if we choose it, we can have more control over the outcomes in our lives than the rest of the suits. Sure, aggressiveness isn't pretty, but it is invigorating and gets things done. Female aggressiveness can protect us from being disrespected and having our rights violated. For example, people may hesitate to cross us because they know that they may receive, at the very least, a crushing comeback.

When we put on our aggressive suit, we have the opportunity to be honest. However, that honesty can get us into trouble. Sometimes people like to be lied to. And if the truth needs to be said, they may want it to come out of an uncertain or mousy mouth. Often, aggressive women have no allies and are often required to apologize for the telling the truth and having the audacity to pursue self-preservation.

Also, the aggressive suit can put a woman at risk for being seen as less feminine, the anti-coquette. And when that "masculine" woman has what is deemed to be too much influence, vengeful people may encircle her. As a result, we women who wear the aggressive persona, often end up betraying ourselves for the sake of peace and the appeasement of someone else's ego; we back down. But then we recoup our anger and go on to assert ourselves again, hoping the next time it will be different…that someone will understand us.

At first, we put on and take off these suits purposefully. This is just like playing dress-up as these are not our real selves. But we come to a point where we just want to get by, or in the case of the aggressive woman, just become angry all the time. We become too emotionally exhausted to take off the suit; we forget we are even wearing it. Eventually, we are no longer able to distinguish between where our skin ends and the fabric begins. We even start to look like someone else.

We have to get back to our real selves by getting rid of junk thoughts. However, like nature, the mind abhors a vacuum. We can not only seek to vanquish our old mindsets; we also have to replace them with better ones.

Focusing on solutions is a good way to start. Instead of lamenting over situations that we don't like, we should take them as opportunities that challenge us to look beyond our supposed limitations and make changes. That includes challenging the negative mind chatter that prevents us from seeing solutions that are often right in front of us. Also, we should have a bias toward the positive. Even when there aren't obvious challenges, bias toward the positive will make us more aware of all the wonderful things in our lives. Focusing on goodness makes it grow.

Be aware that during the process of replacing negativity with positivity, we will have to fortify ourselves, because as we are making those changes, there will be moments of dread. Externally, seemingly insurmountable obstacles may suddenly appear and other things will look like they are falling apart. This is because old mindsets and their corresponding external forms die hard, fighting vigorously to stay alive. They will bombard us with scary images and thoughts about the unknown while pretending to offer protection if we just stay where we are.

"Just put on the suit," whispers the ego. We'll have moments of weakness when we pull the suit out of the closet. But what the ego doesn't tell us is that if we put on the suit, we will be mentally different and quite possibly change physically into a person who is not really us. Our natural, God-given radiance will be hidden under a costume.

When the ego tries to trick us, these are the times when we have to be brave. Brave enough to believe in a greater tomorrow. Brave enough to let go of what is not serving us, despite being comfortable with it. Brave enough to trust that all is and will be well.

COMATOSE

The comatose level not only suppresses the mind like the asleep level, but it also represses. Zombified, the repressed mind is the totally disassociated part of us where we send our most painful, traumatic memories. These memories are stored in fragmented compartments hidden from the conscious mind to prevent us from shattering emotionally. This splintering prevents us from being overwhelmed and is the only thing stopping some of us from taking a willful step to exit this plane of existence.

But this level doesn't only contain our personal memories. It's also the holder of epigenetic trauma carried through bloodlines (Transgenerational Epigenetic Inheritance). The Bible may even touch on this in Exodus 20:5 where the sins of the father are passed to the children to the third and fourth generation.

Our ancestors had the ability to make known various gene expressions. However, they also experienced many hardships. Famine, war, abuse, disease, and torture made certain genes express themselves while other genes went dormant. This occurred one generation after another. And now we are here…the products of inheritance.

Genes that contain memories can be turned on and off, depending on the environment and how we decide to interact with it. For example, siblings inherit *some* of the same genes, but they can have radically different biological outcomes in their lives based on individual choices. This is a clear indicator of how our genes and actions affect our bodies, specifically the states of our beauty and health.

Distinctions must be made between the asleep and comatose levels of consciousness. The key difference is the ability to identify the source of our behaviors. When we are asleep, a trigger can wake us up. With contemplation or therapy, we can locate the source of our maladjusted behaviors. However, unsavory behaviors influenced by comatose level thoughts have hazy origins. Triggers don't even seem to be a factor. These thoughts are subconscious, working on their own version of autopilot, regardless of what is going on externally.

Another difference between the asleep and comatose levels is that we seem helpless to change the behaviors caused by comatose level thoughts. For example, take weight loss. When we lose weight at the asleep level, we may gain the weight back but can comprehend why we regained it, course correct, and lose it again. But at the comatose level, we may gain back more weight than we lost, and our eating becomes a full-blown addiction. No matter how much we want to stop eating, we just can't. Basically, when we have an immovable block, a comatose thought hiding a memory may be the culprit.

Also, another distinction is the comatose level's accompanying sense of false guilt. When comatose, it isn't the true guilt of actually having done something, like at other levels. It is more of a ghostly, accusing voice that says that the cause of the traumatic memory we are hiding is really our fault. Even if the memory is hereditary, somehow, we are still the cause of it because of shared DNA...guilt by association.

So, what's wrong with hiding traumatic memories? Really, who wants to re-live or uncover pain?

Well, to understand why we have to clear the multiple horrors from our psyches, we have to think of a traumatic memory like a tick. A tick attached to our skin is like the effects of a hidden trauma. We may scratch, but if we don't pull off the tick's body, it can cause a systemic infection. And that is if we are lucky enough to even know the tick is there. Sometimes a tick hides on an obscure area of the body. Just like the tick, repressed thoughts and memories produce virulent symptoms. Even though we may ignore, run from, or aren't aware of the cause of these symptoms, the hushed-up part of us knows that something is wrong.

We really do want to be free and clean. That's why, subconsciously, we attract people and events into our lives so that we can purge. But the more of these people and events we invite into our lives without knowing the purpose for their existence, the more pain we experience. We *unknowingly* continue to splinter, and more compartments are created in our minds. These compartments hold more bitter memories that we hide away from the conscious mind. We become more neurotic, aggressive, and self-sabotaging.

Since egos and their accompanying personalities are pretending to be the real us, they don't have the ability to help. At the comatose level, egos seem like they are protecting us at first, but they are really protecting themselves. Egos realize that if we were to confront the pain and break free of the denial of the past, they would die.

In an effort to live, egos build walls around certain events so that we can't see them...those compartments. And if we can't see them, we can't heal them. However, we can feel something is off. But when we seem to be getting too close to the real culprit, egos jump out at us, warning that there is some kind of danger to be avoided, though we don't know what it is.

What is going on between us and our egos is the ultimate love/hate relationship. The love part is that our egos protect us only so we can psychologically function. The hate part is that the same egos have to keep us in pain in order to exist.

We have to ask ourselves if we really want to let go of the problems caused by a comatose state. Surprisingly, we may not. Our splintered minds, under the direction of the ego, have been protecting us from something. That something may have been so traumatic and threatening that it was too hard to cope with at the time. That is why the splintering happened in the first place.

Take an angry woman, for instance. This woman has a reputation for having an "attitude" and being highly aggressive. What is not known is that she has a memory in her subconscious mind as a result of being abused as a toddler. She can't consciously remember it, but the scar is still there, unhealed. Now, in her adult years, her trauma is being directed outward. The ego is basically allowing her to release a pressure valve without solving her real problem. So, if someone speaks to her in a certain tone or disrespects her, the ego tells her to protect herself and she goes off. Whereas spectators see a raging lunatic, what is really going on is a little girl in a grown woman's body trying to receive the protection she didn't get as a baby. Her rage is a cry for help, for something buried so deep that she doesn't even know what it is, let alone how to fix it. If someone tells her to relax and let things roll off her back, that is more of a threat than the awful consequences her rage brings her.

But, like the angry woman, we aren't meant to live at the whims of negative emotions. Healing requires self-awareness of patterns and choosing to fix them. In other words, we have to wake ourselves up, usually without a trigger, through regular self-examination and honesty about our life conditions, particularly, our comfort zones.

Though our comfort zones are familiar, they are often destructive. Comfort zones cause us to unconsciously adapt to chaos, and anything beyond that chaos seems horrifying. We may not be happy in our comfort zones and may even hurt; but we brush all that off as normal states of being. Sometimes we don't know what is best for us and what is wrong looks right, especially if it mimics our hidden pain.

We have to be aware that there are unknowable aspects of our psyches influencing us and accept that we may never know the total cause of our angst, but we can choose different behaviors. Enacting new behaviors may be exceedingly difficult and will take constant effort. We can start by changing our mindsets like at the asleep level thoughts.

Then we claim our innocence through forgiveness. Forgiveness is a major factor in solving all problems. Innocence is our birthright and self-forgiveness is the very thing needed to free us from the guilt that feeds traumatic memories. We don't have to know what we are forgiving; we just have to forgive the effects and have at least a desire to be free of guilt and the unconscious desire for punishment that comes with it.

Not only do we have to forgive ourselves, but we must also forgive our DNA. That may sound odd at first, but we have to clear harmful ancestral memories out of us. Again, we don't have to know what we are forgiving, because we may never know what happened to great-grandma or what she did. However, it serves us to let go of the heartache and guilt that she may have passed on to us.

What we can't forgive, we must ask our souls to do for us. We ask our souls to make room in our hearts for something worth knowing. Our souls know what is going on and also why we carry these sorrows with us. With their superior knowledge, our souls will do what they are supposed to do, in their own time.

Acceptance also helps. We have to accept that our minds hold innumerable memories, and we will never know all of them. Some of these memories are actually multiple memories that have been blended together. So, if we clear one memory fueling a situation, there may be one or a thousand more still operating.

Of course, we wish that all things were easily conquerable. But sometimes, some issues have to be managed day by day, such as hidden traumatic memories. These memories are part of us, enlivening our cells. We may not be able to escape them, but we can strive to manage them. Therefore, management is not failure; it is really success.

At the same time, we must be open to miracles. Spontaneous healing may occur. There may have been a higher purpose for the memory. But after some time, the soul, body, or mind may decide to relinquish the memory for whatever reason.

We also must stay awake (mindful) as possible. Being awake prevents us from creating or "remembering" false memories based on faulty perception or overactive imagination. This takes discernment.

Moreover, an awakened woman knows that not every bad feeling or failure is the result of a comatose thought. Comatose thoughts aren't to be casually scapegoated. In fact, *most problems don't originate from this level as this is rare.* For instance, if we overeat, it is most likely caused by our love of potato chips. If we do not meet our goals, maybe we just aimed for the wrong thing. Bad relationships may be the result of superficial attraction rather than real love. Regardless of the origin of our problems, we are still responsible for our successes and failures.

Finally, if we feel any tension in our solar plexus, that is a reminder that we are in a situation that demands our full attention. Usually when we feel tension in that area, we want to get rid of the uncomfortable feeling by suppressing the sensation and thoughts that go with it. But that knot is screaming, "Wake up!"

So, do just that.

AM I REALLY ALL THAT?

A beautiful, healthy mind is indeed a portal for physical and emotional well-being. And it is by God's design that our bodies reveal who we are.

Lines on our faces show past joy through smile lines or worry through furrowed brows. The rest of our bodies can show dedication to a healthy lifestyle or desperation for acceptance through too-thin bodies. Well-nourished flesh reveals an appreciation for the skin, whereas unkempt, thinning hair may signal depression.

Though there are cosmetic fixes to disguise who we are, it is better to discover the hidden contents of our minds and go from there. Dissecting our minds' thoughts allows for awesome growth opportunities. These opportunities give us the power to dislodge negative mindsets that contribute to self-defeating behaviors.

As we work on our conscious thoughts and release our hidden ones, we will discover that underneath the debris lies a treasure trove of radiance. That radiance is at first mental but then condenses into the physical. Once these mental contents are known, we can bravely accept them, forgive, and make room for something better, more beautiful…and that is the gift of life itself.

SOUL AFFIRMATION

I develop a beautiful mind so I can have a healthy body. I release all the reasons illnesses manifest in me—the memories, ideas, and thoughts that cause me to experience mental and physical pain.
I grieve the past and send it to Heaven for healing. As the hidden parts of my mind are cleaned up, my body is freed, too.

CHAPTER 12

SOUL INTENTION

We were scared, but our fear was not as strong as our courage.

—Malala Yousafzai

The thing we call beauty appears to be hidden within the vibrant colors of a glistening rainbow. However, all too often it seems like the sun evaporates the rainbow before we can even get close to it. And on we go, chasing after another dewy rainbow, again and again.

Since we can't grab a rainbow, we substitute it with material idols that come in many forms. These idols are supposed to be channels through which some kind of beauty can flow. We buy pretty trinkets, find appealing lovers, go on endless spiritual journeys in exotic locations, or indulge in photo-worthy food. Occasionally, we find something that resembles everlasting beauty, and we hold on to it for dear life. But idols always disappoint. Life has a way of snatching the idolized beauty away.

Why does this happen?

The vast majority of what we call beauty vacillates or disappears because we are searching externally for something that can only be found internally. Beauty that has its origin in matter will always be impermanent. Trinkets go out of style, lovers disappoint, some spiritual journeys leave us doubtful, or we end up self-medicating with lovely food. In other words, when we base beauty on a sandcastle, the ocean's tide will inevitably come in and sweep it away. Obviously, we are looking for something else.

This is where intention comes into play. Intention is a conscious decision to obtain and take action to achieve a desired outcome. It is the force that allows us to bring goodness into our lives; otherwise, bedlam would take over. To be intentional is to have a focus and a plan to see that focus come to fruition.

But when we are intending for beauty, we can't implement just any plan. We must look beyond the superficial aspiration and ask, "What is this beauty for?"

We may come up with a list of reasons for why we have to "externalize" our desire, but each word on that list is but a mere symbol of the real beauty we hope to "internalize." But we can't internalize real beauty until we know what that is. Real beauty is the expression of higher values, exaltation of the mind, and a connection to God that is not only believed but lived.

Superior intentions create superior (real) beauty. The soul communicates with you and subtly suggests ways to generate excellence while nudging you away from negative ego-based desires or selfishness, which are inferior intentions. When you're not careful, inferior intentions fill in the gap where you have disconnected from your soul and prompt you to fall back on subconscious programming. You will find yourself creeping toward un-real beauty which is nothing but ugliness.

Ugliness is simply anything that allows the negative ego the opportunity to exhaust the resources of the soul. Ugliness demoralizes and deflates by making us believe we are less than human, that we are animalistic. We go on to tell ourselves lies about our condition because we can't face the truth of what we have become or allowed to happen to us.

Unfortunately, some ugly things are enticing and temporarily soothing; but in the end, these things bring us nothing but disappointment and numb us to the real beauty lingering just beneath the surface. Thankfully, intentional thinking is not dependent on our desire to feel good in the moment. Intentional thinking is all about knowing real beauty exists, even though we may not be able to see it yet.

So, do we want to keep chasing rainbows? I think not. It's time to create real beauty, together. This will be a two-step process. First, we will go past those three ego-based consciousness levels that were mentioned in the previous chapter and try to create goodness from the inside out by being intentional. Second, we will target the loftier type of beauty which is a transformation of the consciousness that aims for beauty of the spirit. The end result is the conquering of the lower emotional mind, overcoming the idea that we are just ordinary, and transmuting our spirits so that we can connect to and behave like God.

THE STATES

Despite having perfect souls, we're still swayed by emotions. Our emotions, influenced by insecurities and lack of knowledge of our true selves, are why we live our lives in at least one of the lower three levels of consciousness (semi-awake, asleep, and comatose). But even when we are thinking at those levels, we still do have a degree of willpower, and that willpower works in conjunction with intention.

However, we don't all share the same thought process or motivating force. Moreover, we receive information, process it, and then react to it differently. Taken all together, these factors are the building blocks of our states of intention. These states are also offshoots of the three levels of consciousness because they, too, derive from the ego-based personality. How and when we move from one state to another depends on our flexibility and what's happening around us.

The ego can actually be used to help us with our states of intentions. True, most of the time, the ego acts like a trickster, especially when we are functioning on automatic pilot. But if we acknowledge our negative ego and corral it, then the ego can be flipped, and its positive aspects can be utilized. At that point, instead of letting the ego run the show, we take full advantage of it.

On their own, the states of intention are like the natural elements of fire, water, earth, and air. Each state reflects different aspects within our psyche. The fire state helps us intend for beauty forcefully. When we are in a fire state, we are zealous and passionate. We are also brave and enjoy taking the leadership role. But we must manage our fire state because dynamism can excite a crowd to build a civilization or destroy with a burning flame.

The water state is the fire state's opposite. While in the water state, we go after beauty in much more subtle ways, usually seeking it in our imaginations first. We have a tendency to lean toward traditionally-feminine emotions to bring about beauty by being gentle, nurturing, and creative.

The earth state pursues beauty in a practical manner. Real beauty has to be stabilized on a solid foundation, so we are all about being practical in our earth state. Also, when we are in the earth state, we like to take our time so that whatever beauty is created will last.

The intellect is the main vehicle for the air state. The air state creates beauty by being highly sociable and actively communicating its idea of beauty to others. Though the air state makes us somewhat detached, we can use aloofness in a rational manner to create beauty.

Despite having all four states within us, usually one state comes to the fore and mingles with our baseline personality. Be that as it may, we were given all four for a reason. Different life situations demand different approaches, and we must learn to bring out all aspects of ourselves. For example, a fire woman, who is intending to create beauty by having a loving relationship with her child, may have to tone it down and allow her water side to come out. On the other hand, a water woman may have to bring out her fire when attempting to create beauty by being an advocate for the homeless.

Switching back and forth between states of intention can be a challenge, but with practice and emotional control, it becomes easier.

Not only are the states of intention important when creating beauty, so is the method. The intention and method should be implemented together. The ever-popular method of positive thinking works for many women. Positive thinkers intend from an affirmative state. When intending for beauty, they use cheerful affirmations and visualize ray-of-sunshine outcomes. This method is best for optimistic types.

However, some women do better with an antithetical approach. They intend for beauty in terms of removing something bad; so, the wording of their goal may be misinterpreted as being negative or dreary. Women like these may be more sensitive, cautious, or analytical types.

Take for example an anxious heavy smoker who is intending for the beauty of a smoking-free life. If she is pressured to make statements like *I am free from cigarettes*, her mind may rebel, and she'll be more stressed each time she makes the statement. Chances are that she will not only have one cigarette before the end of the day, she will have a few packs. It would be better for her to use a release statement. The release statement is used to remove something undesirable. A sample release statement is: *Even though I may desperately want a cigarette now—for the next five minutes—I am choosing* not *to have a cigarette.*

After our states of intention and method have been ascertained, then the level of intention must be dealt with. Our level of intention is *how much dedication we have to maintaining control of our minds when we are stressed.* Certain things make us lose control and unintentionally create ugliness instead of real beauty. When that happens, usually at least one trigger is puppeting us.

On the surface, triggers are uniquely personal irritants that set us off. But they really are indicators of something much deeper. A trigger prompts a reaction that causes us to perceive that a situation is making us feel depressed, not worthy, incapable, and puts us in survival mode. When these buttons are pushed, we can feel like we are losing something valuable such as our sense of safety, security or importance, and we react with hurt, rage, and anxiety.

Usually, the reaction to a trigger springs from the asleep or comatose levels of thought; that's why we do not know consciously why we react to certain situations so intensely. We just know the outcome which is an explosion of emotion and an awful (ugly) situation.

Reactions to triggers have emotional intensity levels, one to ten. Ten is the most painful. However, it is not the trigger that is harmful; it is the damaging reaction that accompanies it. If we find ourselves aroused by a trigger, we should try to stay below a five.

At five, we have the ability to maintain a controlled response, stay in the moment, and be willing to work on a resolution. But five is also a warning that our emotions can overtake us if we aren't careful, and we can unknowingly wind up time traveling to a past event or circumstance—the subconscious origin of the reaction to the trigger.

If we allow ourselves to make it to ten, we are no longer rational and are operating from the unconscious chaos of a trigger. Then only raw pain leads us. The insidious influence of past suffering exaggerates our reaction to current circumstances, with all of our disruptive behavior tragically on display.

These triggers remind us of traumatic events, especially in our childhoods, that left residual pain that we have not dealt with; these are impact moments. We didn't or couldn't properly manage those impact moments at the time, and the memories fester inside of us. Bear in mind, an impact moment wasn't necessarily some big ordeal. It was just a moment that was perceived as traumatic in some way and lingered in the mind.

Past impact moments now define and hold us captive to our past, and the resultant triggers can be called to mind in many ways. We can be triggered by sensory stimuli such as sights, smells, or sounds similar to ones that happened during an impact moment.

When the right stimuli are activated, we can lash out at others for no apparent reason.

Triggers set off sorrowful feelings of not being heard, honored, respected, or loved. Also, they arouse repressed guilt, shame, and fear. Symptoms of triggers can physically manifest when we pester/nag, worry excessively, pick fights with loved ones, are hyper-vigilant, withdraw from family and friends, or become depressed.

There is no way to create beauty, especially in its highest forms, when we are consumed by triggers. The great thing is that triggers can be released. We have to first recognize that we have one or multiple ones. Then we must be willing to explore the triggers' origins. Even though this may very well be a painful process, we shouldn't be afraid of or omit this step.

After we locate any trigger's beginning, we start the process of forgiveness and give up the instant gratification we receive by indulging the trigger. It is also helpful to know how we feel when we are triggered. Our bodies are indicators and will tell us by becoming tense. Tension builds up in our minds, too, (intensity levels one through four), and if left unchecked, we can explode (intensity levels six to ten, especially ten). Momentarily, we feel better as our stress hormones dissipate, and we have transferred our frustration. However, we are left with an ugly situation.

Being mindful of our triggers may not guarantee that we won't instinctively feel angry or fearful. However, we can become aware enough to see how we are associating the present with the past. We can then remind ourselves to remain firmly planted in the present moment and reclaim our strength and selfhood. And that is *beautiful*, when we can turn our pain into our triumph.

THE CROSSROADS

There is an intermediate step between the ego-based and transcendent ways of living. It's called the crossroads. The crossroads is the point where we can choose to stay at lower levels of intention or rise to the highest forms. Though it seems like the obvious goal is to transcend, it's very difficult to do so because of deep-rooted fear.

Fear is one of the main drivers of low-level intentions. It gives us the false belief that we are in control as we maniacally try to manage the outside world. But fear, the deep-rooted kind, never gives us control over anything. It actually overrides our ability to think clearly, hence, blocking higher intentional thinking by creating doubt, to the point it can actually immobilize us with inertia.

We can become afraid of even trying, believing that we can never achieve real beauty and have to settle for superficial substitutes. This leads to stagnation, manifesting anything from our tolerance of a bad relationship, staying in an unsatisfying job just for the money, or accepting unhealthy lifestyles. In other words, ugliness comes to us, even when it is in the guise of something appearing beautiful.

Fear itself also appears to be beautiful. It has a melodic voice and singsongs us away from spiritual purity, which is what beauty ultimately is. Fear says real beauty is not commonplace; therefore, it can't really be known in the everyday world. As we listen to fear, the very thought of real beauty becomes more elusive and frightening.

Moreover, fear knows that real beauty comes at a price. The price is that we'll have to stop depending on those not-so-good things that we love so much. Let's be honest; no one wants to do this. And that's when fear works overtime, telling us to avoid letting go and stay complacent...that certain "things" will save us. But the irony is real beauty doesn't hurt; it brings better things to us—better than what we let go. Fear's job is to convince us that the possibility of a truly beautiful life is not even possible. It wants us to choose to go backward and settle for those delectable idols.

Like fear, we've got a job to do, too. Regardless of what drives our fear, we have to get to the root of it; that's our job. This is so we can understand and reverse the damage that fear has caused. Once we understand how to tune out that fearful voice and press on in spite of all of our internal and external obstacles, we can embrace the changes needed to evolve into more beautiful versions of ourselves. But we have to be willing to shake off the shackles of fear and walk into the unknown with conviction. We really can be free from self-imposed fear and have faith in ourselves and God. We should go full-on and acknowledge the light within.

Sooner or later, we all find ourselves at the crossroads—the place where we start the process of breaking down so that we can be built back up, better than we were before. Once that's done, we can feel the warmth of our inner light and go beyond the crossroads to create beauty on a whole other level.

HIGHER AND HIGHER

Regardless of what the physical world demands from humanity, the soul still uses it to demonstrate itself. We have to assist in that process.

That is why the crossroads is so hard. The power and knowledge granted by the crossroads is not handed out like candy. That "training" has purpose. It weeds people out. Our understanding of the correct use of those gifts must be tested. Even reading spiritual tomes such as the *Bible, Quran, Bhagavad Gita*, or any variety of self-help books is usually not enough to develop any ability to create beauty as God would. For an untested human to yield the crossroads' great power would be a mistake.

Therefore, knowledge is forged through traumatic growth. This growth started at the crossroads is completed at a higher level. And this refinement is not meant as punishment for some sins we committed. It is used to eliminate our negative ego-centered way of life and bring us closer to God.

Even at the highest levels, the use of intentional thinking is not a shortcut to bliss; there will always be some sort of daily trial we must face. We must accept these difficulties and transform them because this is how noble character develops. As we see challenges as opportunities, "Aha" moments come to us, and we can make conscious shifts in our thought patterns. After going through these uncomfortable growth cycles, we may have expanded our consciousness enough to be granted genuine creative power. The purpose of this power is to be used to advance humanity, and energy of this kind homes in only on those who are truly ready to ascend to the spirit's transcendental realm of beauty.

Transcendent beauty goes beyond the states of intention because it is where we become unconditioned beings who are no longer at the mercy of egos and personalities. It goes beyond faith; it is knowledge. We function from an inward precept called godliness, knowing we are made in God's image and have a degree of His power to create. That power is to replicate goodness and beauty as our Maker would. Recreating God's goodness is not an easy task, but knowledge helps us as we learn how to do it. As we grapple with whatever difficulty comes our way, we know that we can choose to see the beauty in the situation or create it.

However, our focus shouldn't be on exact outcomes, a desire for how we think things should be. No matter how high we go, our ego minds will still be with us, and they think they know what the best solution is. We have to release our intentions into the Universe so that the most glorious outcomes can occur. Understand that your intention is not the goal itself. Rather, it sets a compass and gives the direction you should go. The path is composed of thoughts, actions, and motives, and its direction is important because it will lead to who you will become.

If you carry the wrong intention to achieve an outcome, you may not become who you want to be or end up where you want to go. The journey really does matter and its signposts keep us on course. Think about this: What do you look like on your path from afar, right now? Also, to get what you want, are you a taker? If so, be careful because you may have a positive destination in mind, but you won't end up there without being reciprocal to others and the Universe. So, focus on the spiritual nature of the desire and live that on your journey.

However, despite our physical efforts, the only material certainty that is promised is that the Will of God will be done because the entire balance of life has to be maintained. When we allow the certainty of God's material will to occur, we can be assured of the best outcome, not only for ourselves but for everyone.

As sublime as our journey can be, removing the selfish element can be difficult. It's sometimes easier to accept low forms of beauty because they don't require us to be selfless. Low forms of beauty only require submission to the negative ego and its insatiable greed. Journeying, we have a choice between low beauty and high beauty, and there will be many moments when the ego will misdirect us with its signposts. The ego restricts the power of choice by tricking us into believing that its perspective is real and good. If we follow the ego's signs, we'll think selfishness gets us the biggest reward. We'll detour and end up seeing only its warped version of beauty.

Of course, there is nothing wrong with enjoying the material world. We deserve to reward ourselves for a job well done, give lavishly to others, or just have a good time. Those types of things are pleasurable, and if used properly, go a long way toward mental health.

But we aren't here just for a good time. We are here to be an expression of the spirit. We do this by showing ourselves we have faith that our beauty is more than physical and can be so rarified that we can actually speak a version of our word into existence. Though God is the only entity that can create all things, isn't it awesome that He loved us enough to give us that same ability to a lesser degree? At first, we may not believe it. But if we can muster even the tiniest bit of faith, we will be able to claim some measure of real beauty, the kind that God would create.

At the transcendent level, we become a silent one. Silence is what we need to make things happen. God-focused silence is not about being verbally quiet, though. It has to do with quieting the mind, becoming as neutral (emotionless) as possible during unsettling situations or when our faith is low. Silent ones ignore all external stimuli and racing thoughts; they go in the opposite direction. This takes practice because we believe what we see and have a tendency to get riled up emotionally.

Think of being silent like picking up a fork. When we pick up a fork, there is no emotion, just the movement. That is how we have to be in response to unsettling situations, just do what needs to be done without the drama. Be objective, neutral, by removing any agonizing thoughts or even preferences, for that matter. Just suspend the mind for a brief moment. Then, when we are sure our emotional reaction is stilled, we can fill our mind with a thought that reflects real beauty. No, this is not suppression. It is just choosing something else. We must constantly ask ourselves this: *Is my reaction to this thought, person, or situation creating real beauty?* If it isn't, we can peacefully disengage.

Ultimately, silence is a sign of how we really see ourselves— either as a simple human or an extension of God. When we decide to be an extension of God, we rise above it all. This level requires the utmost discipline, years and maybe decades in the making. But when we are there, we don't have to do anything else. Our very presence will be enough to inspire real beauty in others.

DOROTHY'S MANTRA

Remember those rainbows we talked about earlier. Well, there was a girl from Kansas that chased rainbows, too.

The Wizard of Oz is the story of one girl's search for beauty. At first, in her colorless world, she couldn't see the extraordinary beauty that was all around her. She longed for a sensuous beauty, one defined as delight for the eyes. Her ego in the form of a tornado took her to a seemingly beautiful place that had colorful yet deceptive beauty and was filled with saviors, in particular, the great and powerful Wizard. Despite Oz's chromatic richness, which Dorothy had fantasized about, all she wanted was to go home. But in the process, she projected her own inner beauty onto her friends (Cowardly Lion, Tin Man, and Scarecrow). Finally, with courage, she owned the real beauty that her family had instilled in her and declared: "There's no place like home." Clicking her heels, magically, she was transported back to the place where real beauty existed all along.

All the beautiful things we do are really actions of the soul. When the soul is in charge, we don't feel like what we're doing is hard or rough labor. We feel good and our joy makes our souls light up. Our souls are delighted that we listened to them and did the work they called us to do. Ultimately, souls are masters of beauty; we only need to serve them.

Like Dorothy, we also have the ability to take ownership of real beauty at any time. Using our power of intention, we can inspire ourselves toward higher ideals. We can also be guiding lights by demonstrating to others how to release attachments to lower-level beauty and the attraction to ugliness.

We women, when standing in our power, never settle for mediocrity. We are compelled to create celestial beauty. Therefore, we aren't afraid to allow our power to manifest because of fear of greatness and what comes with it. After all, God has given us the power as a key component of our being, and we unlock it with the proper use of intention.

SOUL AFFIRMATION

Intention is not a destination but a direction. That direction puts me on a path of self-discovery. As I journey along, I learn what I really want, why I intended for something in the first place. That is my real desire, my real want, my real need. Sometimes when I arrive at my intended destination, I still want what I originally intended. However, sometimes I do not want it at all, because I received the real prize during my journey.

CHAPTER 13

GROW YOUR SOUL STRONG

For as he thinketh in his heart, so is he.

—Proverbs 23:7

Our bodies are more than just conglomerations of skin, bones, blood, muscles, nerves, and hair. They are actually vehicles that our souls use to express themselves. They have been appointed with purpose, with each one playing a part for the betterment of us all. Hence, it is of vital importance that we take care of our bodies so that they carry out their sublime purpose.

Being so susceptible to mental influences, what we think, our bodies become. Thoughts, both conscious and unconscious, determine what sacred or profane ideals we express or suppress physically. Our bodies morph themselves to accommodate the specific actions the thoughts demand. Hence, bodies are testimonies of how connected we *really* think we are to the Divine, despite what we may verbally claim.

However, no matter how spiritualized we may feel about our bodies, we do live in a world where mundane physicality and conditioned preferences come into play. We've all been at the mercy of cultural standards regarding the body. And we can all attest to how living under someone else's standard is tyranny.

Part of our beautifying process is cleansing our minds of imposed artificial standards. To exuberantly embrace ourselves means to no longer have the lingering belief that we can only be acceptable if others think we are, and we instead love our unique bodies, whether they appear to be pleasing to a large number of people (general public) or are appreciated by what may *seem* to be only a few.

See, it really doesn't matter who deems us attractive or not. We will serve our souls better if we strive to be deliciously lovely only to ourselves on the physical level and pleasing to God on a higher one.

Being beautiful by our own standards and maintaining our health will bring us nothing but benefits. Regarding our purposes, coupled with sound minds, we can use our bodies to be great mentors, too. How? By being proud of our own beauty, we can be positive role models for other women and girls who just really want to love themselves.

YOUR PERSONAL HOLY TRINITY

The body has its own holy trinity. Being holy, this trinity is generative—life-giving—birthing and growing the seed of wholeness. It radiates our best inner qualities, basically our zoetic goodness. That is why the trinity was given to us by God, so that we could discover, develop, and spread that goodness around.

To achieve maximum output, our trinity's part each serve a distinct yet dynamic role to bring about the good. The three parts consist of the mind, heart, and physical body. Generally, the mind (the thinker) is where analytical and critical thinking occur. This thinker is what we depend on when deciding what and how to believe. It's also what we use when making choices based on those decisions. Next is the heart. It deals with the emotional nature, which is highly energetic. The heart is where we develop compassion and love for all things, including ourselves, but it also holds our fears and resentments. The final part of the trinity is the body. The body acts out what the mind and heart decide.

But even in the best of circumstances, sometimes we need a little help stabilizing our trinity. When our trinity are off-kilter, strange and unwanted external equivalences can occur.

A mind that is out of balance tends to focus on negative things by misusing its analytical capabilities and becoming overly critical. And under mental duress, our fear-based selves can emerge. Unsavory strings of personality flaws intertwine, creating a psychically "bodied" shadow in the form of distress such as anxiety or lashing out.

When the heart is unsteady, there seems not to be enough love. We become clingy and seek constant reassurance, or we are so afraid of love that we push it away. Either way, we end up experiencing pain, the very thing we tried to avoid. On top of that, our hearts can suffer from metaphorical love sickness. It's like a virus that infects us with the idea of sorrowful sacrifice. It makes us believe that we are to give too much of ourselves with the expectation of getting little or no affection back.

When the mind and heart suffer, they combine to manifest symptoms in your physical body. Then your body configures itself to match the ugliness carried inside. The three parts go about their business of making your life miserable: The mind becomes reactive and calls it instinct, seeing only danger. The heart loses trust and perceives people as subconscious projections of internal ugliness. And the body performs aggressive actions against friends, making them enemies.

However, a healthy trinity lets you exude a beauty that originates from your soul. The mind reflects an intelligent choice for goodness. Happiness and peace are the primary emotions of the heart. And the body lets you physically love others as you love yourself.

When we think and love properly, we can't help but to want to take care of our physical vessels, and with our well-cared-for trinity, we are able to maintain our connection to God and others without the interference of negative thoughts or emotions. This is what being balanced is all about.

THE JUDGER

The judger accompanies the unbalanced trinity. It causes us to agonize overeating a piece of cake, missing a workout, or not fitting the trendy beauty standard. As enlightened as we are, the judger still whispers to us that we are not enough. It makes us take our guilt out on our bodies, either through shame, contempt, or attempts to severely modify them.

The judger is emboldened by external and internal criticism. Though we use bright-sided methods to relieve ourselves, we just can't seem to get those forces out of our heads. The judger, on the other hand, is pleased with our misery. It rubs its hands together, satisfied, knowing that we have been put in our place. We keep satisfying it by subconsciously scanning for things that reflect our inner discontent, and we definitely have no trouble finding them.

Our eyes are drawn to carefully selected images of unattainable standards, particularly in the media, that match our personal insecurities. Depending on our particular self-doubt, it seems like we can never be pretty, thin, or young enough. For instance, the judger says that your healthy weight is too fat; it is better to have your bones jutting out. Or maybe it's not enough to be so-called average.

We have to remember that God didn't make any of us defective. Therefore, we have nothing that needs to be hidden or shamed. We have the perfect bodies to carry out our missions here on Earth. God loves our bodies, and so should we.

As we evolve, we should transform our perception of bodily perfection, too. Our new perception will strive to see only our goodness. That is freedom.

ALL STRESSED OUT

Now we will focus on the strictly physical aspects of the body by creating great health and maintaining it. However, we'll start at the opposite end of the spectrum by examining a particularly insidious thwarter of health.

The thing labeled as stress is epidemic in today's society. It seems as though we are constantly under pressure, threatened, or overwhelmed. We try to avoid what we think is stress by using all sorts of coping mechanisms...repression, acting out, avoidance, etc. Ironically, we end up more agitated and feeling vanquished. But is that what stress is all about? Are outside forces really to blame for our angst?

Or is the real reason why it is so hard to get rid of stress because we believe that it originates from the wrong place?

We assume the source of stress is outside of us. However, stress comes from inside. Stress is the negative reaction we have when we perceive the exterior world as hostile or burdensome. Therefore, stress is really an internal perception issue. It arises in three ways, all internal. One, stress comes from holding on to the frustration and pain that we are afraid to acknowledge or let go. Two, stress happens when our desire to have things the way we want doesn't materialize and we get something we didn't want instead. Of course, the desire-mind resists that notion and suffers while blaming. Three, whenever we do something we really don't want to do, our inner self rebels and counteracts by making the body feel uncomfortable and tense. The body is trying to get our attention so that we'll feel bad enough to stop doing what we don't want to do. But we don't listen, or we feel as though we don't have any other choice but to continue.

When stress occurs, an internal battle is waged. As we fight ourselves, the body often polarizes to extreme degrees, zig-zagging back and forth, trying to become centralized. At first, we feel this as general malaise. However, if the inner conflict is severe enough, mixed with guilt and anger, the fight-or-flight response will kick in. Over a prolonged period of time, severe disease can result.

One of the disease-causing culprits is cortisol. Cortisol is not bad in and of itself. It is basically a hormone released by the adrenal glands. In fact, during emergencies it can save our lives by making us ready for action. In quieter moments, it gives us a little push to get things done. But the trouble comes when the body's cortisol level remains elevated. This is a symptom of chronic stress.

Cortisol is related to inflammation and some argue that inflammation is the basis for all disease. Moreover, the mind affects the body, too. So, *symbolically*, if cortisol is high and the body is inflamed, what are we emotionally inflamed about? We may have to do some soul searching. But hidden emotional issues, and sometimes not so hidden, need to be addressed.

But as we work on discovering what's in our mental houses, we also do the work on the physical houses. Sometimes the physical work is actually easier than the mental work. Also, the physical may *need* to be worked on first. This is because a high cortisol level has many ramifications on the body that are often more immediate than the damage being done to the mind.

For instance, take excess belly fat. Because the abdomen has more cortisol receptors, fat ends up being deposited there rather easily. The dangerous kind of fat is visceral and surrounds our internal organs. Visceral fat increases the likelihood of diseases like diabetes and can cause chronic inflammation to increase. Inflammation begets inflammation, and the body's immune system responds by releasing cytokines. However, when there are no viruses or bacteria to fight off, we get auto-immune diseases like arthritis.

Cortisol affects the mind as well. It is a major contributor to the breakdown of cognitive abilities. Add to that, mental tension can manifest as head and body aches. Insomnia from an overactive mind can occur, too.

Stress hormones are addictive, and it is necessary to detox from the chemical rush of being agitated. We must stop gravitating toward stressful situations and people. The high we receive from low frequency activities, like gossiping and venting our emotions, has to be replaced with good feelings that come from the opposite. For example, we can reward ourselves with a little happy whenever we turn away from those things.

Also, to maintain our sobriety, we should monitor what we consume with our eyes and ears, particularly in any type of media. Instead of consuming entertaining emotional drugs, we should ingest spiritual and emotional food. We must not "eat" any media, social or otherwise, that makes us feel egotistically better or worse about ourselves.

Meditation, prayer, and relaxation are also great tools to help the body release and avoid the stress high. All of these options ease the mind so that it can more readily accept its connection to the soul. For example, during a stressful time in my life, I chose a twenty-one day, twenty minute meditation bath. This practice allowed me to re-direct my mental focus and release anxiety and worrisome thoughts that weren't serving me. YouTube has many useful meditations available. You can use whichever ones resonate with you. And they calm us when the negativity from stressors ramps up. We can find our bliss anywhere...church, woodlands, a beach, the middle of a bustling city, or even the sanctuary of home. It really depends on where we feel most alive. In these places, we can heal from the onslaught of hormones and emotional carnage.

Finally, there is laughter. We can really find the humor in anything, which is sort of like finding the blessing. We laugh because we know that we have a finite amount of time here. We can use that time to dwell on sorrow, or we can release those feel-good chemicals by having a chuckle. And we can genuinely smile because goodness is always there, no matter how devastating something may appear. It can be difficult to see the good sometimes, but even then, smile anyway. The very act of smiling can trick the brain into thinking we are happy.

Living a less stressful life may take some effort, but it can be done…but we shouldn't stress over it.

COUNTING SHEEP

Sleep is more than rest; it is a source of nourishment. Fully rested (nourished), we awaken with a renewed sense of vigor and optimism. Our productivity and cognitive abilities are enhanced, and our bodies are apt to move more energetically. And as we're bouncing around throughout the day, our bodies are lowering their risks for cardiovascular disease and immune disorders. When night returns and we're nestled in our beds, the antioxidant melatonin is released, and cells repair themselves. Also, though sleep will not be the only factor in weight loss, a healthy weight range can be easier to achieve (and maintain) when we get enough. When we are sleep-deprived, certain hormonal changes in the body can prompt us to take on un-healthy habits. For example, sleep deprivation and weight gain may be signs that we are under some sort of stress, and stress can lead to binge eating.

So, how do you know if you're sleep deprived? A quick indicator is how fast you fall asleep. A person who is getting enough sleep takes around 5–20 minutes to fall asleep. If it takes less than five minutes, basically when your head hits the pillow, then you're most likely sleep deprived. However, the amount of sleep someone needs varies from person to person. But on average, for optimal health, you should strive for 7–9 hours of sleep per night. Avoiding night-time activities that are stimulating and going to sleep before midnight help to ensure that you're getting enough rest.

It may be difficult to pull yourself away from your computer or turn off that great movie late at night, but you need to think about your health. Act like your mom by caring enough to turn off the lights and tuck yourself in. In the morning, when you wake up with a positive attitude and your body feels good, you won't regret the ZZZs you got.

FLUIDITY

We can go up to a month without food but only a few days without water. Water is the main component of our bodies, and we need to consume adequate amounts to function properly, around sixty-four ounces per day. This is because we lose water through sweat, urine, tears, the intestines, and breathing. If we lose too much, we become dehydrated, which can lead to a host of problems, some severe.

As an aid to digestion, water helps our bodies absorb much-needed nutrients as well as helping us in the process of elimination. This cleansing helps to get rid of toxic gunk that would otherwise encourage the formation of disease. Drinking water is especially important for the liver because its main function is to rid the body of waste products that can kill us. There is no way a human can survive long-term without a well-maintained liver.

Moreover, if we are trying to lose a few pounds, water is essential. This calorie-free beverage fills up the belly and makes us feel full, so we are less likely to overeat. In fact, one of the best times to drink a full glass of water is right before a meal. That way, we will not be tempted to gorge like we are in a competitive eating contest. Also, being well-hydrated prevents us from mistaking thirst for hunger and winding up eating instead of drinking. And when we are not dehydrated, we can exercise longer and burn more calories.

Still don't have a taste for water? Well, maybe vanity will change your mind. Water makes complexions glow, reduces acne, and plumps up skin by making it appear more youthful and dewier. Let's not forget the moisture it adds to our mouths so that we can have kissable breath. And who doesn't like a good kiss?

ALL THIS FOR $59.99

It happens to us all. As we flip through TV channels, someone catches our attention. It's a toned woman touting the benefits of her exercise equipment/fitness DVD. The infomercial is jam-packed with exciting graphics, smiling faces, and testimonials from people who went from drab to fabulous. This infomercial, with all the other ones we've seen, ends with a promise…the promise of extreme weight loss and boundless health with seemingly minimal effort. And there we go, running to the phone to order an item whose price tag ends with the ubiquitous ninety-nine cents.

The hard truth is that a healthy body takes mindfulness, self-control, and dedication to hard work. What our infomercial queen is neglecting to tell us is that, with the exception of the first couple of weeks, weight loss is a slow process, generally one to two pounds per week. And that is if we diligently stick with our diet and exercise plan. Also, she is not mentioning that our body may not achieve the same results no matter how much we play the video or that most mornings we really would rather stay in bed.

However, if we want our bodies to be healthy and reflect it, we must incorporate physical activity into our lifestyle; there's no way around it. We should exercise at least three to four days per week at an intensity that leaves us somewhat winded. The trick is finding out what things we enjoy doing so that we stay motivated to continue on. For example, are we inclined toward individual, couple, or group activities? Also, we should assess our current fitness levels, whether we like videos or the outdoors, and if we are a day or night person. We may have to try out different things to see what we like and fits our end goal. If we want to tone and lengthen, something like barre (a combination of yoga, Pilates, and ballet) may be an option; however, we may discover that we love nature and switch to hiking.

After we consider our workout style and the type of exercise we would like to try, we need to know what our body type is. This knowledge will be integral to our success.

YOUR HEALTH IS YOUR WEALTH

Wealth comes in forms other than monetary. With that said, when we think of beauty, the physical body is usually the first thing that comes to mind. As members of the human species, it is normal for us to be impressed by a well-sculpted body, pretty face, or smooth skin. Moreover, regarding the common definition of beauty and socially accepted standards, certain physical features are considered extraordinary because they are rare. Being realists, we acknowledge that as superficial as this is, the currency of so-called physical beauty is real... at least for a short time while we are at a physical peak.

However, skin-deep beauty is a limited, frivolous concept. The fixation on physical beauty has nothing to do with health. It has everything to do with how much attention and admiration can be purchased using the body as money. However, the allure of physical beauty is a depreciating asset that fades over time because it is based on the perception of youth and we spend a lot of "wealth" chasing that. However, because time marches forward, there is no lasting value or worth there.

But if we've learned and remembered that true beauty resides in the inner core of our beings, pages flying off calendars won't affect us too much. When our mindsets are healthy, we focus on real currency, the kind that lasts a lifetime...things like our chutzpah, kindness, humor, etc. In fact, those assets grow and contribute to our souls' wealth.

Practically speaking, being physically healthy puts money in the bank. Instead of vending machines and fast food, health-conscious women bring brown bag lunches to work, filled with nutritious goodies. The money saved goes toward college and retirement funds instead of constantly buying bigger clothes to accommodate weight gain. There is less wear-and-tear on our vehicles when we opt to walk or bicycle to our destinations. Moreover, being health-conscious makes it less likely that money will be lost from expensive medications and missed work from sick days.

Beyond dollar bills, we need to think of our bodies as entities onto themselves and be thankful for the *richness* of being able to exist inside of them and the *wealth* we receive from our experiences we've had in them. Currency like that is similar to an actual current of electricity that enlivens our lives. We sparkle with electric light when we live our best, healthy lives. There may be times when it is rather difficult to be grateful, especially if we've put on a few unwanted pounds and it's affecting our health, or we discover our first crow's foot which is a reminder of our mortality. But there are a few things we can do daily to value the skin we're in.

We can keep a gratitude journal handy and record in it twice a day. Upon waking, we can thank our bodies for seeing us through the night. Then at night, we write about the ways we were blessed to use our bodies. The ink covering the white pages will give us concrete evidence that our bodies are good and that they gift us constantly. This is wealth.

Another way we can develop gratitude for our bodies is by helping others. So many people are in need of kindness and generosity. It is through acts of service that we see firsthand how fortunate we are and can more fully appreciate our bodies for the good work they do for others.

Our bodies love it when we give them verbal praise, too. We must let them know that they make a positive impact on our lives, and thank them for whatever health they have, so that they will want to give us that, more, and better.

The thing about gratitude, though, is that it is not only given to our bodies when things are going smoothly. The time to give gratitude the most is when our bodies get overtaxed or sick. Despite our best efforts, sometimes illnesses occur. After all, no one was promised a perfect life. During those times, we may struggle to see the gift of our bodies, especially in life-or-death situations. But these moments are perfect for summoning gratitude, which will be a choice that takes effort.

If we are having a difficult time being grateful for our bodies, we can pray and meditate about things that our bodies have already brought us. It takes strength of will to focus on the good, but the results are phenomenal.

The task is awesome, but when we express gratitude toward the body, no matter the circumstance, we declare that we recognize its beauty, and we will make the most of the gift of living and promote that everywhere we go. That way, we will indeed spread the wealth around.

To simplify how to be in awed-gratitude for our bodies, let's sum it up with a quote by Ralph Waldo Emerson: *Cultivate the habit of being grateful for every good thing that comes to you, and to give thanks continuously. And because all things have contributed to your advancement, you should include all things in your gratitude.*

SOUL AFFIRMATION

Taking care of my body is a spiritual obligation. My body is a temple given to me to serve God's will. I am only given one precious body; therefore, it is special. The way I nourish it is a direct reflection of how I feel about the life I have been given. I choose to be happy with my life and body. I am thankful for both of them.

CHAPTER 14

SOUL BEAUTIFUL

The beauty of a woman is not in a facial mole, but true beauty in a Woman is reflected in her soul. It is the caring that she lovingly gives, the passion that she knows.

—Audrey Hepburn

Our bodies aren't meant to be jeweled shelves or mere hangers for clothing. Their purpose is to display the beautiful workings within us, symbolically through our actions.

Throughout the book, we've been building up to this particular point: By beautifying our actions, we're creating connections between the mind, body, and soul which allow for internal beauty—soul beauty—to truly transform and take place with-in and with-out of us.

Cleansing our minds, setting intentions, and taking care of our bodies are done for the purpose of performing beautiful actions. It seems like we'd automatically do these beautiful actions, right? After all, who doesn't like beauty? However, sometimes the beauty of an action is hidden. The dirtiness of self-absorption prevents us from seeing it. And sometimes that dirtiness is so crusty, so icky, that we think we're keeping our hands clean by pretending it's not there; even the slightest acknowledgment of its existence has the potential to throw us into chaos.

Chaos is not only the appearance of disorder, but it's also a lonely place. Chaos has a way of exposing us so that we can't run from the truth of ourselves. When exposed, we feel so alone, so naked, and we want to disappear back into our illusions.

But chaos doesn't believe in our false constructs; it only seeks to bring us to our highest good. When our falsehoods attempt to diminish or obliterate goodness, chaos forces those falsehoods to change until they become good. Chaos does this by yanking back our safety nets just when we go into freefall and are mere feet from the ground. But the space between midair and the cold dirt is where miracles happen. A split-second of mindfulness is all it takes to have an epiphany. That revelation enables us to see the purpose of the chaos and accept it. We stop fighting and embrace our grandest purpose which is to be a vessel for the soul and God. Then suddenly, we know what to do and act as though we are a divine being in a human body.

However, before any beautiful action can take place, we have to make the decision to tame the ego-possessed mind. When we are in the dirtiness, the brain cultivates so many random thoughts, but it is up to us to cultivate the noblest ones and use them to execute beautiful actions.

That's why when we are in the dirt, beauty appears to be gritty. But we really do need this grittiness; otherwise, we wouldn't be compelled to change. As we crawl out of the dirtiness, we transform grittiness into action by being brave. As we push the grime aside, we face our pretenses, lay reality bare, and take responsibility for everything no matter what it is.

Without the tenacity grit offers, we may not be able to work through the shame and pain we encounter in the dirtiness. But if we just go through the cleansing process, we will see that we aren't really dirty and that we've never been severed from our souls, the place where we connect with divinity.

Transforming dirty grit into courageousness is faith at work, the knowing that under the dirtiness, beauty is brightly lit. This type of faith is not born of any formal religion. Rather, it is the simple yet fantastic insight that our Creator is with us. It is quiet reassurance and power all at once. It is the spark that ignites action…but not just any action. We're talking about beautiful action.

For an action to be considered beautiful, it can't be transactional. It has to be done for doing's sake. There is no trade involved. The joy that the action creates is all that matters to the performer.

Beautiful actions require a redirection of the mind from the ego, coupled with a desire for excellence. The changing of the mind is driven by a faith that knows no boundaries or impossibilities. It can be induced by repeated affirmation or instruction to the subconscious, where not only pain but also miracles can be found. Over time, repetition of these mantras can yield wonderful results:

I am precious.
I am capable.
I am powerful.

Once the mind is composed, we are free to carry out endless beautiful actions. Physical actions are nothing more than a reflection of what we are internally "being." This is because "being" is not static. Being anything means we are in the active state of "happening." Just by being something, we are getting things done.

Will there be setbacks? It's possible. Will we sometimes fail? Again, it's possible. But instead of thinking that these things need to be avoided, think of them as course corrections.

ACTING UP

The first beautiful action we'll discuss is being graceful. Grace encompasses so many lovely behaviors. Grace itself gives us the ability to control our habitual judgment of others and allows us to forgive them for their errors. It helps us recognize that we occasionally fall short of our highest nature and want the kindness of others' forgiveness, too. When we act with grace, we are complimentary, tactful, and gentle. Our actions fulfill grace's promises of forbearance, warm-heartedness, and longing to make people smile.

Gratitude is also a beautiful action. We should express thankfulness for all the good things we receive, and more importantly, all the good things we are able to give. It must be said that we show some of our most genuine gratitude during our most trying moments. As difficult as it may be to see at first, during those painful moments, there is something praiseworthy. Those are the times when we are cleansed of our dependency on the external world and given the chance to re-discover our inner power.

Another beautiful action we can perform is to respond to life instead of reacting to it. What is the difference between responding and reacting? Responding is when we allow ourselves to influence a situation in an effective manner by using reason and calmness. However, if we are reacting, we are allowing our emotions to become overblown and not creating positive solutions. Responding rather than reacting can take a titanic effort as with most spirit-ascending concepts. However, when faced with a particularly daunting circumstance, we have to disconnect from our emotionally-driven minds and take an objective look at ourselves, not the situation. If we look hard enough, we can see the truth inside of ourselves. And that truth is that we are stronger than the situation and can choose to meditate upon victory instead. Meditating, we realign the soul with corrective thoughts that bring us back to the light where we belong.

Of course, it takes work and discipline to learn how to respond rather than react. But instead of seeing this as a struggle for success, see it as *success using struggle*. We can do this by redefining the meaning of struggle. Struggle in and of itself is not bad. Struggle often accompanies growth because it gets us out of our comfort zones and makes us face our fears. Struggle, therefore, can be viewed as a precursor to success. When we respond to struggle positively instead of reacting, we move forward with the singlemindedness of bringing forth a beautiful result.

The next beautiful action is being happy. Happiness is not an emotion caused by externals. It is a choice first and then a behavior. We start by inducing the mind to be cheery with repeated instruction to the subconscious and then stabilize our efforts with action. *Doing* happy is the opposite of *doing* fear, worry, failure, and anger. Doing happy is making other people genuinely happy. Also, doing happy is making mistakes and laughing about them, having gotten the lesson. Moreover, doing happy is continually brushing off the notion of suffering. As we let go of suffering, we reclaim our innocence. This means acting *spiritually* like an innocent child because every day is a clean slate, and we don't have to wish for purity because we already have it.

However, many times we mistake the feeling of pleasure for doing/being happy. Pleasure requires an external factor, a stimulus. So, if there is no external factor and we don't "feel" what we think happiness is, we mistakenly believe we are unhappy. However, true happiness is always there, and we can do happy at any time, even during the worst of times…oh, how the mind rebels against this. But it doesn't change the fact that in all situations, we can find something happy to "do." We do this by focusing on praiseworthy aspects. If we are ever pressed to find the good, the use of creative visualization comes in handy. Though we may be anxious, we can do our best to visualize a mental scene where we are performing some act of lovingkindness. The scene should initially be as close to what the ego-mind thinks can realistically be achieved, so that the image of a better future and the intrusive thoughts about the present don't clash too much. Incrementally, visualizations can be expanded beyond what the ego-mind first believed was possible.

Along with doing happiness, compassion is another way to act out beauty. Compassion is the craft of being humane. Yes, craft. Crafting is a creative skill and needs repetition to be perfected. Being compassionate creates (brings forth) an atmosphere of sharing. But it takes practice because we have to learn how to let go of our ego-desires by getting selfishness out of the way. Sans ego, we are free to act on our natural empathetic drives. There is no need to attack, because we choose not to have enemies, but instead be sensitive to the needs of others. And if someone seems to be going against us, we can look past their behavior and act compassionately in order to understand their pain and offer our hearts to them.

However, practicing the craft of being compassionate is not always easy. In fact, there will be times when it seems almost impossible. When confronted, our egos will seek to justify our indignation or convince us that being compassionate makes us losers. But our souls always speak and quietly remind us that there is a better way to live. Actually, our souls have been preparing us through past trials and tribulations for moments such as these.

But the most beautiful action is love. Love is an act of service. St. Augustine said: *What does love look like? It has the hands to help others. It has the feet to hasten to the poor and needy. It has eyes to see misery and want. It has the ears to hear the sighs and sorrows of men. That is what love looks like.*

When we perform the act of love, we become transcendent. We rise above earthly constructs and see beyond race, color, or religion because love causes fear to lose whatever grip it has on us. We see the beauty of others as God sees that beauty in them. That kind of love demands an open display of kindness as it cannot and should not be contained or hidden. Hence, when we are doing the act of love, it's impossible to hoard our affection.

Loving connects us to one another. And love, like hate, is a choice like everything else in life. The choice to behave in a loving way frees and uplifts us all, while hate constricts and keeps us bound to lower-level thinking. The soul is enriched by love, while only the selfish and confused ego can benefit from hate. Beauty attaches itself to loving actions; hate can only form gnarly bonds with ugly mindsets.

But let us not forget that our bodies are there to give ourselves love, too. Loving our inner qualities and our bodies is not vanity. It is the actual honoring of our temple, making sure it is not defiled or corrupted by the mental and physical temptations we encounter. We first love ourselves on a soul level by acknowledging our sacred origins. Then we start loving ourselves on a physical level by being mindful of what we eat and drink and exercising our bodies. Taken all together, love is actually quite healing.

Beauty isn't just about poise. Nor is it perfection or popularity by the world's standards. Rather, beauty is grace, gratitude, the courage to be vulnerable, love, laughter, and sometimes chaos, as that is when the most beautiful transformations take place within us.

And, my sisters, remember this: God is not outside of us. All of the amazing beauty we could ever imagine, we already have.

SOUL AFFIRMATION

I have decided not to look outside
myself for validation of my beauty.
No one else should have the power to
determine that for me. When I look in
the mirror, I put on a smile. Some days
my smile will be genuine. Some days
I will still put it on, arguing with my ego
over if I am acceptable or not. But, at
some point, it will be permanently fixed
in my mind that real beauty is the
untainted goodness in me. I will smile,
a real smile, and will not need a mirror
to see the truth.

ACKNOWLEDGMENTS

To my children:

I could spend the rest of my life trying to articulate my love for you. All sorts of words, images, and thoughts would come to mind. And yet, when I reach the end of my life, I know I still will not be able to express what I feel at the depth of my being. My love for you is far beyond mundane expression, but I will try to encapsulate it in one sentence: Being your mother brings me so much joy that I feel like I'm enshrouded by light.

You all have been my teachers. Through mothering you, I have learned so many things. I learned how to be more benevolent, maintain my faith under the most challenging of circumstances, and have a confident yet humble heart. I apply that wisdom to all of my experiences and transform them into enlightenment. I am truly a better person than I was before you came into my life.

Darlings, stay happy and continue to be way-showers to the world as you are to me. You make me a proud mama. I love you with all I have.

To T. Robinson:

You are such a blessing. It has been a fun journey and crazy at times. Thanks for helping me believe in myself. And in the process, I gained a whole new amazing Soul Sister in you. You are such a good woman. Your wisdom is something I admire. You've been instrumental in helping me grow and achieve my dreams. I am deeply grateful.

To my Soul Sisters:

When I think of my Soul Sisters, my best friends, a smile lights my face. If it were not for you, there would have been no way I could have defined the concept of Soul Sisters. I only hope the love I give to you shows my appreciation and deep gratitude.

To Nick:

While we were growing up, we would pretend to be superheroes. Our favorites were Batman and Robin. Of course, you were Batman, and I was Robin. I did not mind playing sidekick because I never felt diminished. You shared your superhero status, and together we were larger than life, basically gods. Even though those youthful days have long since passed, you are still superhuman to me. You are what every sister should have in a brother. You remind me that I matter and being cherished is my right. It is such a wonderful feeling to know that someone has my back. No matter how many years go by, you are still a superhero in my eyes. You will always be my Batman, and I will always be your Robin.

To Bapa:

Thank you for being you. I love you.

To Mike M:

You are one of the most incredible men I know. By your example, you have shown me how to turn any situation into a more positive one. You're a real leader whose calm demeanor guides everyone to greatness. Personally, you help me in so many ways and expect nothing in return. It is my wish that I may offer you, at the very least, half of what you offered me because even half of your generosity can fuel a universe.

To Dad:

I remember being a little girl and looking up at you. You seemed like you were a giant, your head touching the clouds. Yet you still managed to come down to earth and love me.

Now that you are gone, I can still see you in the clouds; but you are not only there. A smooth crooner on the radio reminds me of your singing. The crack of a baseball bat prompts me to think about your days in the baseball league.

There are days I wish I could pick up a phone and call you; I miss that. And I can always go outside and look at the clouds. In their formations, I see you looking down at me…just like when I was your little girl.

To Mom:

There are people in this world who inspire wonder, fascination, and reverence. They possess extraordinary gifts and pay no attention to the bounds of human limitations. But despite all their greatness and glory, they still fall short when compared to you. You are living proof that angels live on Earth. Only an angel can have the otherworldly strength, mystic wisdom, and magical sense of humor that you possess.

But even the most beautiful angels face adversity. Alas, life didn't turn out as you planned, and you had to make some hard choices. You bravely accepted a new reality and the responsibility of being a single mother to four young children. With fortitude born of the spirit, you took on the challenge and used your power to create, teach, and mold good children. But all of that came at a price for you. You sacrificed yourself for us, working so very hard, but you never once complained. Despite the pressure, chaos, and hard times you endured, you were dedicated to giving us selfless care and putting us on a righteous path.

I just want you to know that I saw everything you did, and I am grateful for all that you still do. Truly, I have to thank you for the splendid moments you've so graciously given me…our dance nights, laughs, and talks. You are such a great mother, perfect in my eyes.

With all that said, I am not sure what I would do without you because you are a vital piece of my life. Without you, I am lost. Mom, I love you more than you could possibly know. Thanks for being the angel that you are.

Amore,
Tina

ABOUT THE AUTHOR

Tina Majerle is a Performance and Self-Worth Life Coach, Applied Positive Psychology Practitioner, Speaker, Philanthropist, Podcaster, and Author. She has helped numerous people transform their lives through one-on-one coaching, seminars and courses, public appearances, and her podcast listeners.

As a philanthropist, she supports many non-profit and charities, serves on boards of directors, and has traveled the world with various causes and charities which include Getting Dirty, helping to build homes for people in Nicaragua. She is passionate about inspiring others and changing their lives.

She is a former model who has appeared in many magazines including a *Sports Illustrated Swimsuit Issue.*

Tina is a single mother of four children: Madison, McKenzie, Mia, and Max.

Soul of a Woman is Tina's first book which has been years in the making and a labor of love. She believes women can cultivate beauty, power, purpose, and happiness through understanding your true soulful self which all starts from within.

CPSIA information can be obtained
at www.ICGtesting.com
Printed in the USA
BVHW030042190521
607637BV00002B/245